Becoming A *Love Dog*

From Emptiness to Tenderness

Patricia Flasch

Published by: Leading From the Heart Publishing
2503 Calle de Rincon Bonito
Santa Fe, NM 87505
www.BecomingaLoveDog.com

Copyright © 2009 Patricia Flasch
Cover and interior illustration © 2009 Gabrielle Cinelli
Book design by Maureen Burdock, THEMA
Editing by Cinny Green, THEMA

All rights reserved. No part of this book may be reproduced in any form without written permission from the publisher.

Becoming a Love Dog is factually accurate, except that names, locales, and individual traits have been altered to preserve coherence while protecting privacy.

Printed in the United States of America

ISBN: 978-0-9792219-0-3
LCCN: 2008911807

10 9 8 7 6 5 4 3 2 1

Soul Notes

Dedication iv

Acknowledgments v

Preface vii

Introduction 1

About the Soul Notes 15

Separation Anxiety 21

The Vehicle of Self-Compassion 55

Developing Inner Authority 83

Walking Through Grief 101

When Food Becomes a Substitute for Love 113

The Tyranny of Urgency 141

Effort vs. Inspiration 155

Being Kind to Yourself When Ill 173

The Blessing of Core Loneliness 187

The Soul of Relationship Beyond Our Patterns 203

Conclusion 215

References 221

Information on Patricia's Latest Work 222

Biography 223

Endorsements 224

This book is dedicated to the Ones I Hold Most Dear,
my inner guides Rumi, Hafiz, Quan Yin, Christ, and St. Francis
and to my two beloved invisible service dogs, Grace & Joli.

Acknowledgments

I am aware as I begin this page of appreciations that it does, indeed, "take a village" to birth a book. What follows is a list of the members of my village.

First and foremost, I would like to thank the members of my personal support team who cradled me and my ideas for this book for more than a decade. My beloved husband, David Pease, and Chittak and Amba Caldwell played an essential role in bringing this book and this author forward into the world. Their spiritual and emotional support, as well as the support of Stephani Comi, made all the difference.

Thanks to my husband, David, for reading countless incarnations of the manuscript and taking care of many home and business tasks, so I had time to write.

I would also like to thank David Chittak Caldwell, my friend, web designer, consultant, and right hand person for ongoing editing of this manuscript, without whom writing this book would not have been possible.

I want to honor my three beloved dogs—Grace, Joli, and Rosie—who supported my journey in becoming a writer with their unconditional love and tenderness.

I would further like to thank all the friends, colleagues and clients who read this manuscript in its various stages; Holly Kinley, Karen Ditrapani, Celeste Yacaboni, Kate Dow, Sofiah Ngoran, and Gwen Campbell. I thank Carol Stewart for her listening times. I offer gratitude to Roger and Lisanne Hawkes for their prayers and belief in my dream.

I especially thank Ashisha Mercer for her editing skills and her on-going input as the book progressed. I would like to thank Cinny Green for her thorough and professional editing, and Maureen Burdock for her awesome cover and book design skills. I would like to thank Gabrielle Cinelli for her cover images and heart in offering her talent as an artist.

I would like to thank my collaborative coach, Karin Leonard, for her insight and belief in me. Thanks also to Isabel Parlett, my coaching partner, for her invaluable contribution sharing her "Work on Words" to help clarify my true spirit message and improve my manuscript. I would like to thank Phil Laut for his input on publishing decisions. A special thanks to Tara Andreas of "Dances of Universal Peace" for sharing her knowledge about Sufi mystics.

Special thanks to Shell Goldman who has supported and counseled me for many years. Thank you to Susan Rush my soul friend and spiritual director, Robyn Benson, my acupuncturist, Thom Rogowskey, my chiropractor and herbalist, and Ivan Block, my massage therapist. These folks kept my body and spirit going as the book progressed.

I would like to thank Coleman Barks, and Daniel Ladinsky for allowing me to use their translations of the poetry of Rumi and Hafiz to deepen the manuscript. I thank David Whyte for allowing me to use "The Well of Grief."

All honor to my inner guides, Rumi, Hafiz, St. Francis, Christ, Buddha, The "One", Quan Yin, and Mary for writing through me. I am *only* your *hollow flute.*

Preface

This book is about becoming a *love dog*. The *love dog* concept arose from the ecstatic poetry of the 13th Century Mystic, J. Rumi. For purposes of this book, we will use the following definition of *love dog*:

A *love dog* is one who enters bravely into inner landscapes so that he or she can live with more freedom. A *love dog* is someone for whom the unseen world is CENTRAL. This is the world of love, communion, inspiration, compassion, tenderness, truth, authenticity, emptiness, and the Divine rather than the world of creating victory over another, deception, being right, or amassing fortune and power.

A wonderful thing about this book is that I am taking deeply spiritual concepts and demonstrating how you might work through emotions that keep you from having a more tender relationship with yourself and others. I am offering specific tools for walking the spiritual path with practical feet. *And, this is not a book about religion!*

What Do We Do About This "God" Thing?

What does this book have to do with God? I realize that for some of you, reading the word "God" or even the "Divine" is a complete turnoff. If that's true for you, please pause for just a moment. I promise that I will not try to force my concept of God on you. During my own lifetime I have been a devout Catholic, followed by an ardent atheist, later a tried and true agnostic. Now I am on a spiritual path and consider myself a *love dog*. I have an eclectic and inclusive idea of God, that includes a place for those with the request, "No God, please!"

I spent my first nineteen years as a devout Catholic. I came away from that experience feeling that I had no right to question the authority of the church or to disagree with any of the church's ideas. Then I heard a sermon stating that women do not have the right to make their own reproductive decisions backed up by the explanation that the pope is infallible. This led to a decade of rebellion and atheism.

Since I had been fed a constant diet of God and religion, I reacted by rebelling and walking away entirely. I believe that atheism was a sacred and necessary part of my journey. I respect those of you completely who do not now and may not ever believe in God per se. I do notice that I have had many experiences I would consider sacred with friends who are atheist or agnostic. Sometimes these beloved friends have taught me more about the beauty of nature or helped me to open my creativity in ways I had not imagined possible. I see these friends as having their own path of spirit.

After my atheist period, I was an agnostic for many years. I wasn't sure there was a God, but I was questioning. I didn't know I could come up with my own definition of God. I didn't know that part of maturing on one's spiritual path includes questioning, redefining, reframing, and coming to one's own truth.

Then I moved back into a relationship with Spirit. Not what others said I should believe, but what was true for me, what made my heart sing, what gave life meaning for me. My spiritual path has become the center of my life and work.

I accept and even treasure all the stages I went through in my journey to finding my own relationship with the Divine. I see myself as a kind of invisible minister encouraging the clients and students I touch to find their own truth and to accept wherever they are on their journey. I have no judgment about their spiritual orientation or lack of it. That is their business.

I would encourage you, dear reader, if you are so inclined, to explore what is true for you. It can be an essential part of your growth to decide on your own definition of God (Source, the One, etc.). Your parent's definition, or your rebellion from your parent's definition, will not carry you through. You need your own sweet definition of the Divine and I deeply encourage you to take the time to find it.

Your spiritual orientation, dear reader, is your business. For some of you the word "God" may feel like a small box, rather than a vast and expansive concept. Please translate the word "God" into whatever term or concept works for you. You might find more meaning using Truth, the Universe, Spirit, Nature, Life, the Divine, or the One, to name but a few possibilities. I will occasionally, throughout this book, use the phrase, "The God of your understanding." This is my reminder to you to substitute the words for God that work for you.

All readers are welcome here, and anyone who is attracted to the idea of *Becoming a Love Dog* has an open invitation to take a place at my side as you read this manuscript. *Your idea of a God of Your Own Understanding is what matters most.* It is possible that your definition of God may change as you read along. Whatever your spiritual orientation, I invite you to take what has meaning for you in the pages that follow, and leave the rest.

A primary organizing principal of Leading From the Heart (the non profit organization that sponsors our seminars and publishes our articles and books) is that "the church is in your own heart." In other words, you decide what gives you value spiritually and you decide and are respected for your religious or spiritual value system.

Patricia Flasch, Santa Fe, New Mexico, 10/19/2008

A POEM FROM *THE ILLUMINATED RUMI*

The grief you cry out from
draws you toward union.

Your pure sadness that wants help
is the secret cup.

Listen to the moan of a dog
for its master.
That whining is the connection.

There are love dogs
no one knows the names of.

Give your life
to be one of them.
—Rumi—

(Barks, *The Illuminated Rumi*, p.78. Reprinted with permission)

Introduction

What matters most to me, what always bring tears of joy and a feeling of inner exultation, is the poetry of Rumi.* When Coleman Barks, Rumi's well-known translator, is in Santa Fe at the Lensic Theatre, I sit in the audience in "the great silence" knowing I have come home. Every cell in my body sings in unison with Rumi's words. He touches my heart like no other. Even now as I write these words, my eyes begin misting.

I *knew* the very first time I was introduced to Rumi's poems that he was one of my Teachers and Guides and that his words, in part, had been written to make their marks on my soul.

Rumi's poetry has had an amazing resurgence all over the world these past few years, perhaps because his work offers comfort in times of so much political strife and warfare. He has become a modern day mystic. Rumi's poetry is a spiritual guide for becoming a *love dog* and shifting from emptiness to tenderness.

....

* Rumi's full name is Jelaluddin Rumi, and he was born in the remote town of Balkh, in what is now Afghanistan. He was a thirteenth-century mystic who lived most of his life in Konya, Turkey. Rumi was the head of a Sufi divinity school and held a doctorate in theology. His teacher was Shams of Tabriz who was a wandering dervish monk.

Introduction

My own deeply personal experience is that when I awaken frightened, lost, or grief-stricken, that grief cry IS my longing for the God of my understanding. In the twilight as I rise out of the unconscious dream state into my waking day, I am often longing for God. The loneliness is palpable, and it seems as if it's about some human being I'm missing. I realize I miss *myself* somehow, and I realize I have once again awakened into my longing for God.

> **If you recognize this love dog place within yourself, it is my prayer that the tools and stories in these soul notes will help you live the life you long for.**

Let's look again at our opening poem:

> The grief you cry out from
> draws you toward union.
>
> Your pure sadness that wants help
> is the secret cup.
>
> Listen to the moan of a dog
> for its master.
> That whining is the connection.
>
> There are love dogs
> no one knows the names of.
>
> Give your life
> to be one of them.
>
> —Rumi—

Becoming a Love Dog

When I read that poem, I am deeply comforted. The poem allows me to integrate my morning grief, loneliness, and longing. Instead of thinking I'm separate or feeling ashamed of these early morning visitors, now I can feel honored. My longing for God, says Rumi, IS my connection with God. To me this means I am only in one true state. I am with God, because I am *always* either longing for God or knowing I am connected with God.

To know our grief, anxiety, despair, and the full range of our humanity *does not mean* that we have fallen out of grace with the God of our understanding but rather that the One we call God is present in the midst of our heartbreaking humanity and offers a point of integration that is very comforting on our path.

Knowing God is present while we experience our deep emotions ends dualistic thinking. My belief and experience is that dualistic thinking causes suffering. As soon as we begin to judge, "I'm good" or "I'm bad" or this experience is "good" or "bad," we are already knee deep in suffering. We make life "right" and death "wrong," health "right" and illness "wrong," thin "right" and fat "wrong," white "right" and black "wrong," light "right" and dark "wrong." We are endlessly comparing and judging our experience. This is painful. We have no room for forgiveness or neutrality. Forgiveness and neutrality open our hearts to understanding and compassion, hence, a possibility of a fully authentic life! Without dualistic thinking, our grief cry simply becomes part of our journey rather than something we must overcome in order to return to a place of feeling connected.

My grief, my despair, my loneliness, and *yours* are a part of God. As the Rumi poem says, "Your pure sadness that wants help IS the sacred cup," just as the whining of a dog for its master is the connection. Rumi continues by saying, "There are *love dogs* no one knows the names of. Give your life to be one of them"

What does it mean to be a *love dog*? I'll share what it means to me. And I've asked a few *love dogs* I know, what they would like to say about their own experience of being a *love dog:*

Introduction

My simple and personal definition of a *love dog* is a person who wants God (the God of their own understanding), or inner peace, or truth, or enlightenment, or soul integration, as much as they want water if they are dying of thirst. *Love dogs* are always seeking, always pining, or alternately *knowing* that the most essential part of their lifetime here on earth is this holy connection.

Another *love dog* and collaborative coach of mine, Isabel Parlett,** says that being a *love dog* reminds her of the way our culture views dogs. She says, "Dogs are the perceived symbol of loyalty and unconditional love, and part of our purpose here is to love ourselves the way a beloved dog loves us. Once we do love ourselves with deep devotion, then we can also pass that love on to all those we touch."

My friend and web designer, David Chittak Caldwell,*** says, "A *love dog* is someone who comes from their heart, who wants the best for all, who longs to be filled with love, Spirit, and vastness. A *love dog* hopes to go to that place beyond right and wrong where all is well. They want to love more than they want to be right. *Love dogs* may at times be angry, fearful, or greedy. But there is, within them, a deep desire and willingness to return to compassion and to serve something larger than themselves."

Another *love dog* friend of mine from Taos, New Mexico, Jeannie Zandi,**** a facilitator and soul practitioner, says, "A *love dog* dares not to be right, not to be first, to admit a mistake, to sing off-key, to not defend or justify their behavior. They dare to skip, to laugh, and to pour the love that shines from their heart all over every woman, man, child, and beast that comes into their sphere. A *love dog* is one who dares to be clueless, to not have the answer,

---

** Isabel is a master of the power of the English language. For more go to www.parlancetraining.com

*** Learn more of David Chittak's expertise at www.thevastweb.com

**** To explore more of Jeannie's wonderful offerings, go to her web site at www.jeanniezandi.com

to not be clever, to be caught off-guard, to fail, to not make sense, to give up, to lie on the ground lower than the most low, singing a happy, dopey tune."

I love each of these definitions of a love dog. *For the purposes of this book, we will use the following: A* love dog *is one who enters bravely into inner landscapes so that he or she can live with more freedom. A* love dog *is someone for whom the unseen world is* **central***. This is the world of love, communion, inspiration, compassion, tenderness, truth, authenticity, and the Divine rather than victory over another, deception, being "right," or amassing fortune and power.*

Since I began writing this book, I've been wondering if it's possible to "become a *love dog*" or, if being a *love dog* is innate. Are we born into our *love dog* character or do we unfold into our own deep willingness and *love dog* nature through time and experience and heartache? My experience is that both are true.

On the one hand, I recall that the moment I met my husband—after he drove up in his rusted out green Mercury Comet in Seattle—and I met his eyes, I knew he was a *love dog*. His bright blue eyes took in the whole landscape, and his eagerness in running across the lawn to meet me resonated deeply in my soul. I already "knew" him in some utterly unspoken yet very real way.

My first thought was, "Hmmm, I'm going to marry him." That he is a *love dog* has turned out to be so true. He is always willing to learn, to get help when we need it, to play a sport he's never played, to take a class he knows nothing about, to read poems late at night, to hold both my heartbreaking humanity and my large spirit in his arms. The rugged places in our nearly quarter century union have been worked through precisely because we are both *love dogs*. It is our deepest intention to work things out irrespective of the process we go through in facing ourselves in order to sustain our connection.

My beloved husband says, "A *love dog* is someone who *can* see the forest for the trees. A *love dog* not only thinks outside the

Introduction

box, they don't see the box. A *love dog* knows their own foibles and seeming failures, and loves themselves and you anyway."

About ten years ago I was taking a weekend seminar entitled "Abundance and Gratitude" and a wonderful man stood up and shared his feelings. I *knew* when he stood up that I wanted to work with him. It was a very compelling feeling—like I *must* work with him or I am *supposed* to be his "soul coach."

Though this dear man was very busy and it took several phone calls to get our first appointment, I was relentless. This, by the way, is not my style. Usually one phone call is enough, and if the potential client is not available, I bless them and let go.

This time, I had this feeling that we "belonged" together. At this point in time we have been working together over the course of a decade. Every time we meet, I experience communion. He is a part of my heart as I am part of his. We don't have a traditional coach/client relationship. It's more like *love dog* meets *love dog*.

My dearest friends will walk through fire when we need to work something out between us. My closest friends have an eternal love for me (and I for them). Their consistent message is that *it does not matter* what I am experiencing—the darkest night, the worst experience, the greatest terror. They simply listen and offer compassion. If they think I am off course, they speak up about what they see.

The soul and business coaching clients that I have worked with for extended periods of time, often several years, also have that *love dog* quality. They have a willingness to look deeply at their lives, their humanity, their divinity, and all phases of their process. They take our work directly into their lives. Part of their spiritual practice is to take the tools we work with into their lives and businesses on a daily basis.

It doesn't matter to me, on a given day, if a client is heart broken, lost, or in despair *or* if they show up feeling connected and capable of profound movement in their journey. Either way I get to work with a willing *love dog* heart or I get to enjoy their momentum. I am as happy to be with them when they feel "broken" as when they are experiencing "wholeness." Either way, we are *anamchara*—a Celtic word that means "soul friend."

I've been describing the ones who come by their experience of being a *love dog* naturally. As long as I've known these folks and in all the interactions we've had, they come from truth and willingness. Our meeting with an open heart in that *love dog* space continues to expand all aspects of our lives.

> *Love dogs* use every situation in their lives to make them more: more connected, more authentic, more self-knowing, more devoted, more AS A SOUL. I love working with *love dogs*. It makes my heart sing. It touches my soul very deeply.

There is another category of folks who enter my practice. They are a bit crusty and closed when we begin. Given how thick the veil seems, I often wonder if I should be working with them. In the first few sessions it seems as if their fear is bigger than their Essence. Since my client profile is *love dogs*, I ask myself, "What am I doing here? Why am I working so hard to encourage them to put down the sword and listen to their own hearts?"

For these folks, though, a miracle begins taking place after only a few sessions, or perhaps a few months. I find that while they could not initially let me in or let love in, it was a cover for a sweet heart. These clients begin to step away from their role in the world. They no longer see themselves as company presidents or vice presidents or ministers or counselors or small business owners. Instead they are showing up as souls. They start looking behind the face they show to the world and begin to look more deeply at what is going on inside.

Their introspection, by the way, does not diminish the roles they have in the world. In fact, most of them become much

Introduction

more skillful in their careers, better friends, more compassionate, more deeply connected partners, and more a part of the larger community. Perhaps these folks are "latent" *love dogs*. In other words, they are *love dogs* in their very nature but it had been covered over with human condition so that they forgot. Perhaps these people didn't arrive here on planet earth as *love dogs* but a miracle or a shift in perception has taken place, and now they are *love dogs*.

Both *love dogs* that arrived on earth in this state of profound willingness and deep open-heartedness and the *love dogs* that quickly unfold into those willing hearts with just a tiny bit of coaching are blessed beyond words. To care primarily about one's enlightenment or one's connection with the Divine IS a wonderful gift, and an essential way to create a truly sacred relationship with yourself.

On a much deeper level, I sense that clients fall in love with me as their teacher. But I am just an outer reflection of what they are really falling in love with: a deep, wise, compassionate part of themselves, their Beloved, the God of their Understanding. I don't say this from an egoic position. I say it as a *love dog* on a mission here on earth: to search for My Beloved in everyone I encounter and in every experience I have. And I *know* there are many like-minded souls who join with me in this Invisible Ministry.

The third category I'm aware of is those souls who are not *love dogs*. These are the ones who want to be right. These are the ones whose fear is, at least in this moment, so much greater than their love. These are the ones to whom, in my capacity as a psychospiritual counselor, I suggest that "blame" is their biggest issue. They are lost in who is "right" and who is " wrong" and cannot or will not put down the sword. These folks are not showing up as *love dogs* at this point in time.

Whether they are interested in self-blame or blaming one another, they are not interested in taking responsibility for their experience. When a client or a student cannot or will not see their partner's pain and perspective as equal to their own, then they are not operating from that *love dog* place. Karen DiTrapani,[*****] a shamanic coach from the Boston area, says it beautifully: "There are those who have so many pain pictures they do not have access to their *love dog* nature and cannot howl to find their pack."

That is not to say that we *love dogs* never visit the blaming place, but rather for *love dogs,* blame of self or another is temporary. A *love dog* keeps working on his or her self until the blame recedes and self-respect and respect for one another returns.

I believe that every single soul on earth beneath EVERYTHING is a *love dog,* but some of us have veils that are too thick to pierce. Sometimes when I work with a client I can turn myself into a pretzel to deliver a soulful message that they really can't hear. In those cases, my greatest act of tenderness is to honor their perspective and to let them go with my blessing.

It's unkind to attempt to force willingness because willingness cannot really *be* forced. One of my own greatest blessings is that grief and turmoil brought me to my knees at a very young age. Wayne Muller has written that a painful childhood can leave a positive legacy (Muller, *Legacy of the Heart: The Spiritual Advantage of a Painful Childhood*). In my experience, that's true. We can take our early heartache and be broken by it or it can make us more caring, thoughtful, empathetic, and strong. Pain often leads to willingness. We can use that pain to become *love dogs*.

Love dogs use every situation in their lives to make them more—more connected, more authentic, more self-knowing, more devoted, and more *as a soul*. Becoming more, and more of a *love dog* is a life-long pursuit. It takes skill, patience, intention, tenderness, integrity, support from others, and most of all, willingness. I love working with *love dogs*. It makes my heart sing. It touches my soul very deeply.

[*****] Go to www.sapientiarosa.com to find out more about Karen and her work.

Signs of Being a *Love Dog*

A longing for something nameless

A yearning for something vaster than the small self

A desire to see past right and wrong (Rumi: "Out beyond ideas of right doing and wrong doing there is a field. I'll meet you there.")

An honoring of our own and each other's heartbreaking humanity

A passion for truth

A desire for healing

An interest in tenderness

A deep integrity

A bodhisattva: one who agrees to come to earth to help and serve until all souls are healed, starting with themselves

A deep interest in living authentically

Easily moved to tears or laughter

Life has become a spiritual path

A willingness to learn from every painful experience, turning dross into gold

An intention to stop blaming self and the other

A commitment to forgiving oneself and one another eternally

A mature capacity for introspection

Becoming a Love Dog

My Hope for this Book

This book is written in homage to and for *love dogs*. It is written for those souls who are willing to expand their consciousness. For that reason, I call each chapter a soul note, a message from my soul to yours. This collection of soul notes is a response to a call from *love dogs*. Each soul note is an outpouring of my desire to offer you, dear reader, support to live your life more fully, tenderly, honestly, skillfully, passionately, and authentically. It is my personal passion to join hands and hearts with all the *love dogs* who are yearning for a constant conscious connection with the Divine and are sincere about exploring their own emptiness and want to create a more tender relationship with themselves.

As humans, we so often get caught in the worldly trance—in making a living, raising children, political unrest, and social chaos—that we lose sight of the *love dog* within. We are not always loving, honest, giving, and compassionate. But within us, like a pole star, is the desire and willingness to return to love, compassion, authenticity, and communion. This longing will always carry us back, eventually, to Love. This book offers practical tools to shift out of our unconscious patterns into our true nature, our *love dog* nature.

If you recognize this *love dog* place within yourself, it is my prayer that the tools and stories in these soul notes will help you live the life you long for.

Introduction

Lost *Love Dog*

When I have lost my connection
with myself
and with You,
(the Holy One inside)

I feel such a sense of profound loss.
Life has no meaning.
The compassion I usually take for
granted is dead *and*
my emptiness is larger
than the loneliest and longest winter day.

I am in hell,
like the story
where we arrive at a wonderful banquet
with every kind of delicacy
a truly abundant feast
only to find we have no
hands to feed ourselves.

In my isolation
it seems that everyone around me
is effortlessly putting together
a jigsaw puzzle.
And I have lost my puzzle piece.

Ships passing in the night,
Captains sleeping at the helm,
Moon clouded over,
Waters dark and murky.
Yet my soul resides somewhere in the great silence
expecting the sun to rise
as it has after so many
other dark nights
and waiting in a longing
prayer without ceasing.

—Patricia Flasch—

I would sink and drown a thousand deaths
to glimpse your lovely face.

—Julianna Simon—

HIS LIPS UPON THE VEIL

He has never left you.

It is just
That your soul is so vast

That just like
The earth in its innocence,

It may think,
"I do not feel my lover's warmth
Against my face right
Now."

But look, dear,
Is not the sun reaching down its arms
And always holding a continent
In its light?

God cannot leave us.
It is just that our soul is so vast,

We do not always feel His lips
Upon the veil.

—St. Catherine of Sienna—

(Ladinsky, *Love Poems from God: Twelve Sacred Voices from the East and West*, p. 200. Reprinted with permission.)

About the Soul Notes

It is one of my fondest desires that each soul I touch by this writing, in private sessions, or in seminars receives a practical and portable set of self-help tools to help move toward their own *love dog* nature.

I want you to feel empowered to work through your unconscious age-old emotional pain and memories so that you can experience personal freedom and full creative expression.

I feel deeply grateful to the countless personal growth teachers that have inspired me through decades of transformative work. I would consider my circle incomplete if I didn't pass on the gifts they gave me that have been filtered and integrated into my own heart and mind.

This work is my personal contribution to inner peace and, therefore, world peace.

This book is based on a collection of soul notes. Each one stands on its own. Feel free to skip around and start with those topics you feel most attracted to. This chapter gives you a brief outline of what each soul note is about.

As we open our hearts to this book on *Becoming a Love Dog*, our first soul note is **Separation Anxiety**. It comes first because honoring and healing our sense of separation from ourselves and the Divine is the heart of the core of our work as *love dogs*. We simply must get in touch with our disconnected places and our fear of being alone and find our way to making a lasting connection with *The Ones We Hold Most Dear* and ourselves. This soul note is a map leading you to your inner home.

In **The Vehicle of Self-Compassion**, I offer the metaphor of the car diagram as a way for *love dogs* to begin sorting out both our wisest and most troubled voices. I begin the journey of sharing how we access our own innate wisdom and compassion and come to embrace our own humanity. We cannot, absolutely *cannot* make wise choices about our careers, marriages, health, or any other thing unless we know who is speaking. In other words, are we coming from our wise, intuitive selves (front seat) *or* from our unconscious, troubled selves (back seat)? If our decisions come from the front seat, our lives will work much better and feel much more fulfilling than if our choices come from the back seat.

In the soul note **Developing Inner Authority**, we examine how to step away from external authority figures (political, religious, or parental) and move toward the kind of authority that comes from within our deepest selves and is aligned with our true value system. To be a *love dog* means that we strive to individuate from family systems and cultural influences. When Rumi advises, "Wherever you stand be the soul of that place," he is encouraging inner authority.

The next soul note focuses on **Walking Through Grief** as a beautiful part of our spiritual adventure. I have wrestled with a lot of grief in my own life. I have learned to welcome grief more, so that grief is a more balanced part of my inner world. This has led to more aliveness, joy, and presence.

I meet countless *love dogs* for soul coaching sessions and in seminars who are deeply grieving and who are beating themselves up for their grief. I use these pages to demonstrate how we can embrace sorrow and, therefore, go on living and loving more passionately and more authentically.

When Food becomes a Substitute for Love is a heartfelt look at how we use food (and other addictions) in an attempt to stuff our emotions. When we use food to avoid the big black hole inside, we grow emptier. When we use food as a soother rather than becoming our own kind friend, we are like a rat in a maze. This soul note offers some simple steps to forgive, love, and heal ourselves within our addictive patterns.

The next soul note is **The Tyranny of Urgency**. When we live our lives and work from a place of great urgency, it's as if we have no "pause" button. We are living our lives on speed dial. We become like locomotives flying down the tracks at breakneck speed completely oblivious to the NOW moment and the beauty of the journey. This impulsive feeling becomes a kind of adrenalin addiction, and we become bonded with the feeling of urgency.

When we go through our days centering ourselves and inviting grace to be our partner, our work becomes effortless. We begin to breathe in union with the pulse of the Universe. We become a part of the fabric of life itself and that has a profound impact on the quality of our lives. When we slow down, peace becomes possible, within the inner being of the *love dog*.

The next soul note, **Effort vs. Inspiration**, shows what happens when *we try hard and drive ourselves to make something happen*. The coveted goal we've made may in fact happen, but the road we took to get there has worn us down and we cannot appreciate the accomplishment. We often just make another, harder-to-reach goal, because by then we've become addicted to serial goal setting and the adrenalin surge that often accompanies it.

This supreme efforting keeps us obsessed with the goal, dismissing the pleasure and potential ease of the journey. When we push, we forget our *love dog* nature. One of my favorite teachers, Susan Rush (no joke), always says, "Hurry hinders holiness."

When we work from inspiration rather than effort, grace and tenderness become our allies and our results are often more beautiful than we could imagine. It's not, by the way, that we don't necessarily reach our goal if we stop pushing, but rather it's more like the difference between snowshoeing and snowmobiling. When we snowshoe, we notice the natural setting we're in, we pace ourselves, we strengthen our muscles, and we slow down. In snowmobiling, we're often racing, grinding our gears, and rushing to the next location. It's up to you to decide how you want to get to the mountaintop.

The next soul note is on **Being Kind to Yourself When Ill**. I discuss that when we experience physical illness, we often simultaneously experience emotional pain and self-criticism. We make healing so difficult when we are being machine-gunned by self-criticism. We heal best while resting in the sanctuary of loving-kindness. Imagine lying in a sick bed, really struggling, and someone walks in and begins shouting at you to "get it together, get up and get going, stop whining, pull yourself up by the bootstraps, and get the hell back to work!"

It would be shocking to be treated with so little respect and such blatant verbal abuse. Yet, we often speak to ourselves this very same way when we are ill. Our self-criticism sabotages our healing process.

This soul note delivers clues that point us towards developing more tenderness for ourselves and our beloved bodies. We are invited to learn how to coach ourselves through physical and emotional pain and distress. We want our *love dog* essence to wrap us close during difficult physical and emotional times.

The Blessing of Core Loneliness is very close to my heart. I experienced a personal transformation in writing this soul note that has lasted through all the months since. By boldly sharing the loneliness that has "dogged" me through life, I have set myself free from the shame of loneliness. Perhaps by recognizing your own deepest loneliness you will free yourself from the shackles of the shame of your lonely parts. That is my prayer.

The final soul note, **The Soul of Relationship Beyond Our Patterns**, gives you an opportunity to look inside my soul marriage and witness the great delight that is possible when we live beyond the limiting mental and emotional patterns based on the past. If we really don't know what's possible in our most primary relationships, it will, indeed, be difficult to create the kind of relationships our hearts often long for.

Dedicating our marriages to the healing of each partner creates a richly rewarding experience. When we come together in partnership, truth, and depth, our marriages become living, breathing, beautiful things.

One of the purposes of personal growth is so that we can experience sweetness and harmony with one another. Peak inside. Perhaps you'll like the view.

In closing this introduction, I reaffirm my true purpose statement. What really matters most to me in my work life is this: "I am welcoming the most willing souls on earth, the *love dogs*, into a partnership based on truth and tenderness so that they can leave their caves, stand in all their glory, and celebrate with their tribe." These soul notes are my written expression of my desire to walk in this *love dog* partnership with you.

Just Sit There

Just sit there right now.
Don't do a thing.
Just Rest.

For your separation from God
Is the hardest work in this world.

Let me bring you trays of food
And something
That you like to drink.

You can use my soft words
As a cushion
For your
Head.

—Hafiz—

(Ladinsky, *The Subject Tonight is Love - 60 Wild and Sweet Poems of Hafiz*. Reprinted with permission.)

Separation Anxiety

I'm writing this soul note because *love dogs* need to know about *separation anxiety*. I believe separation anxiety and our fear of being alone is at the heart of our separation from ourselves and God; we need to know how to deal with it and how to find room in our hearts for it.

So many of us are afraid of being alone, and so many of us shame ourselves for our fear of being alone. It is essential in fostering a sacred relationship with ourselves to work through our fear of being alone. There are many others of us who have never considered the issue of separation anxiety. Here are some questions to ask yourself to see if separation anxiety might be playing a role in your life:

- Do I use food, alcohol, drugs, sex, work, or other distractions to fill up an empty place inside?
- Am I unable to leave an unhealthy relationship or situation because of my fears of not being able to make it on my own?
- Do I keep myself company with people, activities, or the television?
- Do I avoid silence and being alone?
- Do I feel disconnected from myself, the Divine, or the rest of humanity?

Separation Anxiety

Separation anxiety may have started very early in our lives. Remember when we were little, how frightening it was to have the night-light turned off? Think of the panic a small child can feel in a crowd of people when they realize they have lost their parents.

This soul note is about how our deeply abiding fear of being alone can turn into separation anxiety. We'll be examining how all the losses and heartache in our lives have contributed to this separation anxiety. What we'll discover is that this fear of being alone is a SURVIVAL issue. Somewhere, deep inside our beings, is the memory of being *little kids who actually would not survive if left alone.* As adults, we sometimes believe the childhood thoughts that arise telling us that if we are alone, we will die.

Together we will find ways to come to terms with our fear of being alone. Once we have become aware of our separation anxiety and taken complete ownership of it, we can begin to forgive ourselves for our fears of being alone. Once we find room in our hearts to love ourselves in the midst of the times we are afraid to be alone, a transformation takes place. The inner place where we remain connected with ourselves and our Beloved is the place all *love dogs* pine for. We are all trying to move closer to our truest selves and further away from separation in any form. My deep prayer is that this soul note helps with that process.

As we heal our inner scars and devote our hearts to the discovery of the Divine, we find beauty, tenderness, passion, sweetness and love of all kinds. It's equally true that when we crack open to the Divine, all of our deeply unresolved issues arise. All those issues that keep us separate from the Divine show up for healing. They shout, "ARE YOU GOING TO LOVE ME NOW?"

I'll begin by defining terms. Because this book is written in honor of *love dogs*, it's important that we share a language so we can work together to heal our inner turmoil. What is separation anxiety? It is the place where I feel separate from myself, you, and my God. In many ways separation anxiety is a huge, at times insurmountable feeling of not wanting to be alone. This fear can be so strong it becomes almost a compulsion to avoid being alone, at all costs. Wikipedia defines separation anxiety as "an excessive fear of being alone without the subject of one's attachment." I see that a core part of our heartbreaking humanity is separation anxiety. For me personally, separation anxiety is the "heart of my core emotional issues."

From a traditional perspective, separation anxiety is actually a normal stage of development for babies that begins at about eight months of age and increases until thirteen to fifteen months, when it usually starts to decline. If there is some kind of trauma in our early developmental years, we are likely to have late onset separation anxiety.

Young children have an experience that is called object impermanence. Object impermanence means that if the ball goes behind the couch, they do not believe the ball is there. When their parents leave the house, they don't know that they will return. Plus, a child does not have a sense of time so a few minutes alone can seem like an eternity. Object impermanence is a setup for separation anxiety. In addition, childhood losses, death, divorce, violence, abuse, and neglect often lead to feelings of separation anxiety as adults.

> **Alcohol, food, sex, or drugs become the primary relationship and the way we avoid feeling loneliness.**

In the late 1980s and early 1990s, when I was studying rebirthing*, I learned that most of us experience a form of separation anxiety at birth when the umbilical cord is cut. After nine comfortable, warm, and contained months inside our

---

* Rebirthing is a connected breathing process designed to help heal past emotions and create more aliveness in the present moment.

mother's womb, we are pushed out into the world and the physical connection to our mother is severed.**According to rebirthing philosophy, when we are born and the cord is cut we begin our lifetime of feeling separate from other (in this case mother), separate from ourselves, and separate from God.

Adult feelings of separation anxiety may range from mild discomfort in being alone to really being unable to be alone without having an anxiety attack. This fear may be a kind of nervousness, shaking, filling up our time with people and things we don't really care about, or it may become an addiction to food, alcohol, drugs, relationship, or work. This separation anxiety can be so serious that it could require hospitalization or setting oneself up to somehow never be alone. When we can't handle being alone, it's impossible to create an intimate adult relationship because our partner will feel hostage to our fear of being alone. When we cannot really "be" with ourselves, and touch those parts that feel most broken, empty, or dark, we also step away from being a *love dog*. A growing tenderness for ourselves is the path to create tenderness towards others.

> **Learning to love ourselves in the midst of our humanity—when we can't handle being alone, when we are using a substance of some kind, when we can't face ourselves in the dark of night—IS a part of what we are doing here on this earth plane.**

I'd like to temper this by saying that we do not have to heal all parts of our separation anxiety in order to be in healthy relationships, but we do need to identify our own issue and have

---

** It is now a common practice to wait several minutes, until the umbilical cord stops pulsing, before cutting it. Some medical practitioners, such as Dr. Sarah J. Buckley, MD, even suggest leaving the cord and attached placenta several days until it naturally falls off. For more go to www.sarahjbuckley.com.

support for working it out. It helps if we have a compassionate partner who is also working on himself or herself. Whether or not we have a partner, we still need to become aware of the fear of being alone, be able to forgive it, and be willing to offer the fear to the Divine for transformation and healing.

I believe that the symptoms of most addictions are rooted in separation anxiety. I have heard many alcoholics, relationship and sex addicts, overeaters, and drug addicts talk about being unable to face that "big, black hole inside." Alcohol, food, sex, or drugs become the primary relationship and the way we avoid feeling loneliness.

I want to be careful to discuss separation anxiety from a place of curiosity and tenderness rather than judgment and criticism. Picking up the baseball bat and beating ourselves for whatever symptoms we may have of separation anxiety will not help. In fact, clubbing ourselves will add a layer of self-shame and can deepen the anxiety.

Separation anxiety is a part of our heartbreaking humanity. Fear of being alone and avoiding the big black inner hole IS honorable because it is part of our humanity. Learning to love ourselves in the midst of our humanity—when we can't handle being alone, when we are using a substance of some kind, when we can't face ourselves in the dark of night—IS a part of what we are doing here on this earth plane, and is equally part of moving from emptiness to tenderness.

Most of us are capable of loving ourselves when we have managed to get an addiction under control. We are able to be kind to ourselves when we are courageous, bold, and able to face our worlds, both inner and outer, with a spring in our steps. When we most need our own love is when we are afraid and compulsive. That is the time to **decide** to love ourselves anyway, right alongside the fearful places.

Separation Anxiety In My Own Life
I'll share my story because it seems to work best if I write to you from the ashes of my own life. My own separation anxiety began in the process of being born into this world and then deepened in childhood with the death of my father and subsequent emotional loss of my bereft mother.

My father's death when I was seven was a cataclysmic event in my young life. For me, because he died so suddenly and in a kind of "unnatural" way (by being crushed underneath a planer machine at the factory he worked in), it was like an earthquake. That day will always be etched in my mind as the day my world came apart—an emotional and spiritual turning point of tremendous magnitude. I found out that something was wrong when one of the nuns at school told me I was needed at home right away.

I remember walking home thinking, "Wow, I must have been a really bad girl this time." Then when I got home, a neighbor came over and said that everybody was at the hospital because my dad had been hurt at work. I waited at home for the rest of the day (I assume under the care of an adult. But, I don't remember.) Very late that night my mom and grandparents came home and I thought they were laughing, but it sounded like they were saying, "He was lost", "He was gone," "He died."

In later years, I realized that what sounded like laughter was really hysterical crying. I remember being in a daze and walking around the room trying to comfort everyone and telling them I'd pray for them. This is sad to me, that I was offering comfort when I, too, really needed comfort.

My mother's devastation at the loss of her husband was really at the center of our lives; it was monumental. I was also terribly confused because my mom was right there but she was not the same mother I had known, and her heartache superceded her ability to offer comfort.

I see, in retrospect, that not only had she lost her soul mate;

she was now responsible for raising four children on a high school education and almost no savings. My mom remained in a trance about the loss of my dad that lasted her whole lifetime.

My loss of my father seemed to be smaller than my mother's loss of her husband, and I missed my dad the way you miss air if you can't breathe. My father's death became an "unaddressed loss" and the loss that colored my entire existence.

Today I have only compassion for my mother *and* my precious seven-year-old being. I write this soul note as a tribute to my beloved parents and as an offering for everyone's losses and grief.

My father's death and my mom's heartache meant that I lost both parents in an instant. This left rips and tears in my inner world. I no longer felt safe. My fear of being alone and the subsequent anxiety became my emotional bottom line. Separation anxiety became the way I viewed the world from then on.

Fear of being alone and separation anxiety have been main themes for me throughout my life. My dad's death split me open into a place where fear of being alone and separation anxiety have been frequent visitors in subsequent years.

Now is a good time for you to pause and reflect for a few moments on how your own early losses might still be having an impact on your life today. Whether your parents divorced, or had addiction issues, or incompatibility problems, or were emotionally unavailable, or simply had to work a lot; whatever happened when you were young, is likely still having an impact now. The lens through which we look at the world today is truly colored by what happened in our history.

This is not an excuse to stay "stuck" in history; it is rather an invitation to consider the role history may be playing, so that that knowledge empowers you to act further on your own behalf today.

I no longer feel shattered by that early loss, and I have truly found room in my heart for myself in the face of that loss. I share my story because I *know* it often helps *love dogs* to touch their own heartache by relating to mine; another situation where *love dog* meets *love dog*.

As an adult, I had another profound loss—the simultaneous loss of my career and my community in Seattle. I'll share the outline of this rather complicated story.

I worked with a partner to create a six-month intensive training that we were to co-lead. I enrolled most of the students for the training from my private practice. As the training progressed, it became the focal point for a spiritual community. It was also my sole source of income.

Then my training partner took over the training. I was not yet in my personal power, and I allowed this—even supported it. He then took the training in directions I did not like or support. I took time for a personal retreat and realized I had projected on my partner all of my unresolved feelings about my father as well as making him into the "pope." I had unconsciously given him all my power. I had completely lost my own sense of inner authority. (See the soul note, "Developing Inner Authority" for more.)

I realized that my training partner and I had "irreconcilable differences." I decided it was time for me to walk away. This was very costly, emotionally, spiritually, financially, and every other way. In fact, at the suggestion of my "teacher" (co-leader, business partner, and "pope"), David, my life partner, and I had separated.

The good news is that when I realized what I was doing, I knew I had to stop the unhealthy projection. I had the strength to walk away. I have been so much clearer throughout the course of the rest of my life not to project unresolved parental feelings on anyone and to demote anyone I start to make my "pope." I am very grateful for the lesson.

The unfortunate part was that when I walked away from the training I also walked away from my community and my career, which I believed was my truest expression of service in the world.

> **It was at this moment of David's shining compassion and friendship that I decided, "I will one day marry this man. He has seen me in my darkest hour and given me love and caring. I will not find anyone with more kindness or more loyalty."**

I realize now that losing partner, community, and career re-traumatized the loss of my parents. These simultaneous losses really had the impact of exposing my raw underbelly. They brought up both an unconscious feeling of deep separation anxiety and put me in a place of post-traumatic stress.

One of my bittersweet memories of that time was the moment I decided to marry David. Shortly after I left the training and my community, I was walking around Green Lake in Seattle late at night. I had already walked the three miles around the lake twice and felt too nervous to stop and unclear about where I would go or what I would do. It was about 3:00 am. It felt like I was falling into a void and could not grab the rails on the way down. The amount of emotion I was experiencing was so overwhelming that I couldn't get a grip. (That's really saying it mildly.) In retrospect, I see I was having a melt down that could easily have become a nervous breakdown.

I stopped at a phone booth just as I was about to go around the lake a third time, and I took the risk of calling David. We hadn't seen or spoken to one another for about two months by that time. I remember telling him that I was sorry for calling at 3:00 am, that I had to leave the training I had been co-leading, and that I was really beside myself. I couldn't stop weeping.

David was very kind. He could see that I really was unable to be alone though I didn't realize that fact at the time. He told me that he was my friend and that he'd come, *"Right now,"* to Green

Separation Anxiety

Lake to pick me up and take me to his home. He told me that it sounded like I needed someone to take care of me and he would help me until I could get on my feet. He also said that I didn't owe him a relationship or a commitment of any kind; he would just be my friend and help me get through a rough time.

It was at this moment of David's shining compassion and friendship that I decided, "I will one day marry this man. He has seen me in my darkest hour and given me love and caring. I will not find anyone with more kindness or more loyalty. That's enough for me."

I am offering this personal story as a potential window for other *love dogs* reading this book to see how childhood loss leads to adult separation anxiety. While a part of me is embarrassed to be sharing this tender and painful memory, another part of me *knows* there is healing in writing about this for me and also for you because you and I are *One* and my healing IS your healing. One of the common *love dog* denominators is the ability to share one's soul truth *even when* it doesn't look pretty.

After spending some time at David's apartment, we began to realize that this was more than just a tough night I had to find my way through. It was the beginning of a three-month period of time where I couldn't tolerate being alone and where I was in post-traumatic stress without really knowing it. I remember that the therapist I began to work with at that time told me she felt I had a "double depression." She described this "double depression" as a situation in our lives when past trauma, i.e., the loss of my dad and his livelihood, crosses over with a current event of similar magnitude. Once one is doubly depressed, it's very challenging to treat the depression. Over time, though, I did find my way through. It was essential that I got top-notch professional help outside the context of my relationship with David.

A few days after I arrived at David's apartment, I called him at work to tell him I now realized I couldn't handle being alone. I didn't mean I couldn't be alone that day. I meant that I was so frightened that I couldn't be alone *at all*. I didn't know how long it would last. I assumed it was permanent. We had a short discussion and he agreed to come home and let go of his temporary accounting job. While I felt ashamed then of being this needy person having to ask for help, I also knew I could not do this any other way. I needed support.

In the years since then, there have been times that we actually look back with fondness on that period of time when we were chained to one another for days on end. *Our bonding as a couple was cemented by my heartbreaking humanity, in the form of separation anxiety meeting up with David's deep compassion.*

Thank God the separation anxiety episode wasn't permanent. It was simply that the core emotions that were coming up around my earlier losses were too much for me to handle. I feel sad writing about this now. For many years I could not have written about this because of the shame I had about not being able to be alone. Today I have a great deal of compassion for myself and I am rather amazed at how well I've functioned most of my life given the childhood loss of my parents.

Often, when I discuss our human condition and our unconscious mind (the back seat of our inner cars), I mention that our critical parents and wounded children have a positive intention.

The part that I love about our history together is that the positive intention of my separation anxiety (to be connected with others), and revisiting my wounded little girl, helped form the bond that David and I have today. When I was walking around Green Lake in the middle of the night, I could palpably feel my separation anxiety move me toward connection; benevolently force me to reach for someone's hand. When David so lovingly took my hand, in my moment of greatest need, it confirmed the intuition I had the first time I saw him that he was my soul husband.

Separation Anxiety

I've often wondered, particularly at that time and the first few years after we reunited, if we were just poster people for codependency. This may be true in one context. And, on the other hand, we have a glorious marriage. We both support and honor one another's greatness, gifts, and talents, and we are both capable of being with one another in our darkest hours.

Had the entire context of our relationship been this extended visit with separation anxiety, we would not have had the strength and skills to build a solid marriage. Instead, we have devoted our lives, as many *love dogs* do, to building and sustaining a marriage of equals that lasts through time.

I don't want to give the impression that I have never revisited separation anxiety again in our twenty-four-year marriage. What is true is that I have never revisited separation anxiety on the level I experienced it so many years ago in Seattle. The fear of being alone is a relatively rare and less intense visitor today because I have so many skills to work with when it arises.

One part of my skill set is that I am able to welcome the arrival of separation anxiety as an old friend, rather than as an adversary. I am likely to have kindness in my heart when I realize history is showing up once again in my fear of being alone. I am filled with tenderness and an ongoing capacity to forgive myself and thus offer the process to the Universe for transformation and healing. I don't dread the reappearance of separation anxiety since it's really just an opportunity to do more clearing. As I do more clearing, I believe it has an impact on everyone I touch.

I once spontaneously mentioned, while giving a lecture to 200 students at the University of Colorado in Boulder on Personal Empowerment, that my own needs were so great, if they were typed on single-spaced sheets of paper, they would extend from Boulder to Denver. I heard a resounding gasp coming from the audience and a brave female student raised her hand and asked, "What does neediness have to do with the topic of personal empowerment?" I don't remember my exact response, but I do remember my inner knowing that we cannot really be powerful without connecting with all aspects of ourselves. I remember thinking, "We aren't powerful from an outside-in perspective, but rather from an inside-out perspective." It was a genuine surprise to me that so many students came up after the lecture thanking me for honoring parts of ourselves we often keep hidden. I also received more fan mail from this lecture than any other up to that point in my career.

Allowing neediness to be a part of our human range of emotions renders us more authentic and therefore infinitely more powerful human beings.

In order to resolve our fear of being alone (or any other core need), we need to find our way to a place of mercy and compassion for ourselves. *And* we need to develop inner strength and the use of tools and resources so that we have a strategy for living on the other side of separation anxiety. The soul note, "The Vehicle of Self-Compassion" will be helpful in developing these resources.

I am reminded once again of one of my favorite Rumi poems where the message is to celebrate whatever we wake up with in the morning.

Rumi speaks directly to the hearts of *love dogs*.

> Today, like every other day,
> we wake up empty
> and frightened.
>
> Don't open the door to the study
> and begin reading.
> Take down a musical instrument.
>
> Let the beauty we love be what we do.
>
> There are hundreds of ways to kneel and kiss the ground.
>
> (Barks, *The Essential Rumi*. Reprinted with permission)

Separation Anxiety

An Example of Separation Anxiety Starring our Rescue Dog, Rosie

Since I'm writing in the name of *love dogs*, I will share a story about a real dog. A few months ago we were at PetSmart when they had animals up for adoption. The pets from our local shelter were being paraded around the store so that shoppers would have a chance to meet the dogs one-on-one.

We noticed a teenage girl walking along the aisle with a golden lab who looked like she had just had puppies. The golden lab seemed both mellow and friendly. We took her for a stroll around the aisles and then took her outside for a while.

We were still missing our beloved dog, Joli, who had died about six months previously. We didn't know this then, because we were unconscious in that moment, but we picked this golden lab because she gave us the feeling that we could replace Joli.

I asked David to step outside without the lab, so that we could have a conversation and not act impulsively. David was already in his own little spell about wanting to please me. So we drove home with the two-year-old female lab wriggling excitedly between us.

For the first few days we had a glorious time bonding with Rosie. We took her swimming, learned that she could play fetch and that she knew all her commands. She was also completely housebroken. We couldn't imagine how anyone could have let this beautiful dog and her litter go. We were clueless.

On the third day, we decided to go out for dinner without Rosie. She started getting nervous and pacing as soon as she could see I was picking up my keys and my purse. As we got towards the door, we could see the panic in her eyes.

We spent some time talking kindly to her and reminding her we would be back very soon. We were not sure what would happen, so we placed her in the kitchen behind a gate held in place with two sturdy chairs. We gave her a bone and a blanket with our smells on it.

> **Each time Rosie struggles with her profound fear of being alone, she is mirroring an older part of me that still lives in my psyche. She offers me, on a daily basis, an opportunity to be kind to her, and in my kindness, to take another pass at forgiving myself completely for my fear of being alone.**

When we returned home an hour later, Rosie had broken down the gate and was pacing nervously around the room and then running into my home office to bang her head against the stained glass window in the door in an attempt to get out. She behaved as if she hadn't seen us for years and years. We now know that lots of shelter dogs, and dogs who have been traumatized or spent much of their lives in kennels, come with a case of separation anxiety. Rosie has great difficulty being alone. She is happy to be with a neighbor, another friend, or one of us, but she can't, as yet, tolerate being alone.

I find it interesting that I'm writing this book for *love dogs* and the need for this pivotal chapter about separation anxiety was first brought to my attention by my dog, Rosie. I think she was brought into our lives as a Divine Messenger just at the time that I was to write this soul note.

Each time Rosie struggles with her profound fear of being alone, she is mirroring an older part of me that still lives in my psyche. She offers me, on a daily basis, an opportunity to be kind to her, and in my kindness, to take another pass at forgiving myself completely for my fear of being alone.

The truth is that Rosie IS me and I am her. We are *One*. She mirrors my own separation anxiety and fear of being alone. Rosie, by the way, is also *you*. She is a poster dog for the potential healing of separation anxiety. Looking into the face of her raw need is looking into the face of my own heartbreaking humanity.

Separation Anxiety

Reminding myself that I am one who paces and bangs my head against doors when I cannot tolerate being alone, offers another layer of letting go.

While it is true that Rosie and I are *One* and that she reflects my own separation anxiety, it is equally true that Rosie is Rosie. She has her own connection with Source, her own resources, her own dog conditioning and divinity, and her own issues that she's working with. Rosie's separation anxiety is both current and profound. My separation anxiety is primarily historical and relatively easy to work through today. I don't have wild eyes and I'm not banging my head against the glass door when left alone. Rosie does represent a much younger and much more wounded part of me. It is important to be able to sort out what is and is not your business and what is and is not the other's business.

> **Here is an idea. Perhaps being needy is not like being an ax murderer, perhaps being needy is just part of our brokenness and its part of what connects us *love dog* to *love dog*, heartbreaking humanity rubbing up against heartbreaking humanity.**

You and I, individually and together, can truly take responsibility for our fear of being alone, forgive it, love ourselves when in it, and offer it to the Universe for transformation and healing.

We've decided to do what we can to help Rosie integrate her fear. We are coaching her to adjust to being alone by leaving her for small amounts of time and telling her clearly when we are going and when we'll return.

When she behaves as if she hasn't seen us for ten years on our return, we simply don't give her anxiety attention. When we don't feed her separation anxiety, we are offering her an act of love. As she calms down, we praise her. We give her homeopathy and remind her every day that she has her own connection with

Source and that she will remember that connection in time. We don't know if Rosie understands our words, but we do have faith that she gets our tone and our good intentions.

Rosie is in the process of healing her separation anxiety. Some days she does well, other days she's beside herself when we get home, but she is learning to trust our love and our consistency. We are also teaching Rosie that she lives in a world where she is loved by many friends and neighbors. Perhaps our dear golden lab, Ms. Rosie, should receive credit for co-authoring this chapter.

I do believe the reason many folks cannot work with a dog or cat that has separation anxiety is because they have not faced their own separation anxiety. It is hard to look into the face of that much raw need and find the heart to call it loveable.

Perhaps being needy is not like being an ax murderer, perhaps being needy is part of our brokenness and it is part of what connects love dog *to* love dog, *heartbreaking humanity rubbing up against heartbreaking humanity.*

I believe that as I continue clearing my own separation anxiety, Rosie will be healed, at least in part, by being in my presence. And she is making progress. Rosie, in three short months, has gone from only tolerating being alone for five to ten minutes without going crazy, to being able to handle being alone for two to three hours. When we were new together, her upset and excitement on our return lasted fifteen to twenty minutes. Today it takes about five minutes for her to calm down. That means Rosie is coming to terms with her own fear of being alone and finding a way to tolerate that fear for longer periods of time. It also means Rosie, as my reflection, tells me I am doing well with my own healing around my personal separation anxiety and its hold on me.

I want to be clear about the two different, yet equally powerful ways we are working with Rosie's fear of being alone. First, we take many opportunities to look in her eyes and say, "I'm so sorry, Rosie, for your fear of being alone." And Patricia, "I'm deeply sorry for your fear of being alone that Rosie is demonstrating. I'm so sorry. I love you. Please forgive me. Thank you."

Then, we remember that Rosie is also her own soul; she's a redwood tree, deeply rooted in mother earth. She has her own connection with Source (we often tell her, Rosie, DOG is your Source.) She has her own resources, internal and external, her own dog condition and divinity, and her own connection with Father Sky.

We both forgive Rosie and ourselves completely in the midst of her fear of being alone *and* we see her as her own strong being that we are coaching toward wholeness. We have a plan to help her return to her strongest, most connected self.

Separation Anxiety: a Soul Coaching Client and My Inner Work

I have a client who is learning to become a *love dog*. We have been telecommuting for the past few years, and I'll call her Shelly. She has been a web designer and is currently starting her own design company.

Shelly's background is that her parents divorced when she was five years old. Her mom remarried and then divorced again a few years later. Shelly is a gifted designer, a brilliant woman, and is good at taking care of herself in the world. She also has a case of separation anxiety stemming from her childhood and two divorces. She doesn't feel she can count on a man to follow through with her. Most of her experiences with men have been short lived and full of pain.

Shelly entered our coach/client relationship for two primary reasons. The first was that she found herself becoming over emotional in a variety of situations and she didn't know what was causing it. The second reason was that she was dating a married man and wanted to take a look at that. (Not that she felt ready to end her relationship with the married man, but she wanted help in taking care of herself within it.)

What I see for Shelly is that many of her out-of-the-box emotional expressions had to do with repressed grief and anger. They also had to do with her loneliness and separation anxiety that is rooted in being an only child who was left by two different dads.

Dating the married man is, first of all, a consequence of her history. She does not feel she can count on a man. By dating a married man, she tries to protect herself from the kind of vulnerability she witnessed in her mother. He's unlikely to leave her since he's already married. I know this is a kind of twisted logic, yet I totally understand how Shelly's reaction to her past trauma and its irresolution in her, led her to this action.

Remember that for me all emotional work that comes up for the client in our relationship is also *my* emotional work. An emotional issue may not be as big for me as for the client, but it's there, even if it's just a whisper of the way it used to be for me and the size of a thunderbolt for the client. As I continue to forgive myself for the times in the past I dated married men, Shelly receives my forgiveness process in her soul and begins to heal on a whole other level. Though I have not dated married men for more than a quarter of a century, there are still residual places in me from that experience of being with married men and my non-forgiveness of myself that are being addressed now.

Most therapists and coaches think that what we are supposed to be doing is fixing, healing, or uplifting the client. I think that's true, but I know I have to do it by first healing myself. Clients are healed by sitting in the presence of the depth of my compassion for myself, which is transmuted energetically to them. Clients also do their own deep emotional work in the process of forgiving themselves. Together we are a powerful force!

Shelly and I have made considerable progress in helping her to learn to pause before expressing inappropriate emotions. We've also been working on how she can communicate clearly and assertively without being passive or aggressive. We've spent many sessions helping her to see how her past pain is connected to her present situation. To the extent that I pause before acting out and to the extent that I communicate clearly and assertively, that same level of healing becomes available to Shelly.

Shelly continues to date the married man and I am filled with compassion for her situation. I believe the underlying reason she is not prepared to let go is because if she lets go she would re-experience the profound loss of both her biological father and her second dad. She's not prepared to go there. She doesn't have the skill set yet to process the original grief. She really is not able to consider being alone, even though there are many ways she is already alone. Shelly's separation anxiety is holding her in a compromising position where she can't move toward a man who would be loyal and consistent with her.

Shelly is committed to her healing and I believe, over time, her growing relationship with herself will strengthen to the point that she is internally married to herself. She will become loving, committed, and devoted to herself. Once that happens, it could open up her life and her relationships.

> I embrace *them* as redwood trees with their own roots connected to Source, their own resources (whether they use them or not), their own humanity and divinity, and their own connection with Father Sky.

It's not my job to influence Shelly's relationship decisions. It is my job to help her become the strongest, clearest, wisest woman she can be. It is my professional responsibility to sit in my own meditation offering forgiveness and compassion to myself for my own "married man history." Together, Shelly and I are healed through the process of forgiveness and offering our human condition to the Divine.

Both Shelly's and my own healing takes place through two primary pathways. The first path is self-forgiveness and for that I'm currently using *Ho'oponopono*. This transformative process is a modern adaptation of an ancient Hawaiian healing technique. It was popularized by Dr. Ihaleakala Hew Len, a clinical psychologist and shaman who helped to heal an entire ward of mentally ill criminals in the Hawaii State Prison system using *Ho'oponopono*. He would simply sit with the files of the inmates, saying inside himself, "I'm sorry and I love you," and a whole institution was transformed (Len and Vitale, *Zero Limits*).

So, I say inwardly in Shelly's presence:

Ho'oponopono, Ho'oponopono, Patricia.

I love you, dear woman.

I'm sorry this old residual material about dating married men is showing up for healing.

Thank you for bringing it to my attention for healing.

Please forgive me for the heartache I caused you in the past, when you dated married men.

We offer this to the Divine for transformation and healing.

And I coach Shelley to use her own form of *Ho'oponopono* so that she can work diligently to forgive and release herself.

The second foundational process that I do in Shelly's name is "the redwood tree process." I mentioned this process earlier in reference to Rosie's healing and I will expand on our understanding of the process here:

Each day before I begin working with clients I take ten minutes to connect with myself. I imagine that I am a redwood tree sitting in the midst of a glorious redwood grove. I envision that my roots have grown deep and wide into rich soil and that I have a profound connection with mother earth. I see that my branches spread out and touch Father Sky. I feel my own deep connection with Source (as I define Source to be) and that I am surrounded by a plethora of awesome resources. I also remind myself that I have my own humanity and divinity. Then I remember the clients I will see during the day and I embrace *them* as redwood trees with their own roots connected to Source, their own resources (whether they use them or not), their own humanity and divinity, and their own connection with Father Sky.

While we are *One*, we are also beings here to do our very own discovery process. I can both have deep compassion for the issues the clients bring forward and see that these issues are a part of me *and* see that their issues are truly their own work, not mine. It is crucial that we recognize our *Oneness* with the other's humanity and that we see that we are also individuals in that we each have our very own work to do, on whatever level we need to do it.

These two very different focuses are both important to our discussion of separation anxiety. Experiencing our unity with everyone else, nature, and the Divine is the healing of separation anxiety. *Ho'oponopono* helps me experience that everything I experience "outside" me I also have within me. We are O*ne*. That oneness exists fully and beautifully at the spiritual and soul level. And yet we need to be careful here. We also live in a world of apparent separation. Each of us is given our own lives to live, with our own decisions to make and our own consequences to reap. We want to allow everyone to live their own lives and to not lose our lives in their business. Boundaries are needed for a life well lived. The redwood tree process helps me keep appropriate boundaries.

Within my work with myself and all those I touch, I use both the *Ho'oponopono* process so that I am full of mercy for myself and the *love dogs* I am working with *and* I remember they are redwood trees with their own amazing strength and resources.

In working with clients, and you, dear reader, I hope to provide 1) deep sanctuary, which *Ho'oponopono* provides, 2) challenge of beliefs and actions that are not working, and 3) action steps to move away from past wounding and toward personal and/or business goals. This is why I call myself both a Soul Whisperer and a Business Catalyst. Starting with "The Vehicle of Self-Compassion" (explained in the next soul note) I offer tools for you to experience your own mercy and tools to build a plan through which your deepest desires can be manifested in the world.

Separation Anxiety Within Relationships
In reflecting on separation anxiety within relationships, I realize that most, if not all, of the couples I counsel have fear of loss/separation anxiety issues. For most of them, it is a core issue. They may not know how to be together in a mutually satisfying way, but the fear of being alone outweighs their marital strife by miles.

I have been with couples who hate each other, but can't leave. Leaving would re-stimulate other losses that they haven't grieved or come to terms with in any meaningful way. This is a sad thing. These couples need the internal willingness to do the individual work necessary to face past losses and to deal with the fear of being alone. If not, they are destined to continue this painful pattern.

> Most, if not all, of the couples I counsel have fear of loss/separation anxiety issues. For most of them, it is a core issue. They may not know how to be together in a mutually satisfying way, but the fear of being alone outweighs their marital strife by miles.

What follows is a case study of a couple staying together in part out of fear of loss and unresolved separation anxiety issues. We'll call them Celia and Greg. I met Celia and Greg a year ago when they came in for counseling because they felt they were always on the edge of breaking up and because Greg had an unresolved alcohol issue.

Celia is about seventy and Greg is sixty. Her background is that she has had serious clinical depression that began when she was about thirty. She also has some health issues related to aging and her fragility. Celia is quite able to do her emotional work and is getting stronger as we go along our journey.

Greg is a Vietnam Vet who has not received support to deal with the post-traumatic stress disorder he got from being in the war. He uses alcohol to try to suppress those painful memories. He thought that since he'd been willing to give his life for his country, he would return to the United States receiving the hero's welcome he deserved. Greg has not, as yet, been able to fully recover from the cultural abuse of being spat on when he returned from Vietnam.

Despite what they are up against, I do believe this couple loves one another. Even beyond the fear of being alone and their separation anxiety issues, they care deeply for one another. They are *love dogs*.

As is the situation for many Americans right now, Greg lost his job a few years ago due to downsizing and this further shattered his self-esteem. Another way that Greg has been shutting out his suppressed separation anxiety issues is by gambling. At this point he's lost most of his life savings and retirement.

Celia is beside herself. Given her age and her own history of depression, she really can't risk losing Greg. It seems logical that she should consider leaving Greg. He drinks, he gambles, and he takes chances that dramatically affect their financial future. Most of us think we'd leave Greg. Yet, she can't leave Greg. She loves Greg *and* her fear of being alone would only re-stimulate a deeper depression.

I support Celia in staying with Greg. Not that it's my choice, but because I see her position emotionally and I trust her knowledge of herself. I am not saying this would be a good decision for anyone else. I am also not saying that Greg is 'bad' because of his unresolved issues. I am saying that they love one another and the fear of loss, the fear of being alone, for both of them, looms much larger than the other difficulties they face.

While I am encouraging Greg to get treatment for both his gambling and drinking problem, I can also see deep in his soul eyes that he has a tender heart. I can't really help Greg to do his core emotional work on separation anxiety because alcohol is in the way. That issue would first have to be addressed in order for us to proceed. I can, however, continue to address my own addiction issues, which have an effect on Greg's soul. As I release my food addiction, and face the underlying issues behind that, I do so in my name *and* in Greg's name.

I don't see Celia as a victim. I see her taking a stand for self-preservation at this moment in time. It remains possible that Celia will change her mind about staying and it is possible that Greg will get the treatment he needs. Whatever happens with Greg and Celia, I continue my prayer without ceasing for forgiveness of this portion of my own unresolved humanity that they mirror.

While I don't *know* this to be true, I do believe that Celia and Greg's heartache of feeling separate from themselves and one another is part of something deeper, a feeling separate from and a longing for what they may not even be able to name (God, Source, Life, Nature, the One, the Isness, as you prefer.)

I want to thank you all for opening your hearts to my own story and the stories of Rosie, Celia, Greg, and Shelly. I applaud your courage in peeking in to the big black hole with me.

On the Other Side of Healing Separation Anxiety

At this point in my adult life, I feel good about being alone most of the time. In fact, today, I crave alone time. When I don't have enough alone time, it makes me a little crazy. I look forward to times within every day where I can be with myself. I look forward to those times within my marriage when David is off pursuing his own interests.

> We have a marital vow that says, "We promise to go on living and loving with all our hearts after the other of us has passed on." The only way for me to keep that promise is to accept, forgive, love us both, and offer to the Universe my fears for the future.

We just decided a few weeks ago that David will go to all of the four men's weekends the Men's Wellness Conference offers in New Mexico this year. We agreed that this is a good time for him to do what he loves: connecting and socializing with other men in the process of healing. And, it will be a wondrous time for me to be alone.

David also decided to become politically active in the 2008 election. This involvement will require lots of hours. What that means to me, today, is that all those hours are free for me to do with as I like. I may join him at some of the meetings, but I am joyful about his pursuit of his own political interest.

Since David is eleven years older than I am and men often (though not always) die younger than women, I am working now on loving and forgiving myself for the grief cry that may be coming my way. Whoever dies first, there will be an opportunity to find my way to the place where I know I am connected with the Divine even through and after death. This is likely to be a bumpy road and I will wonder some of the moments whether God has dropped my hand or not, yet I will remember, as time goes on, that God does not ever really drop my hand no matter what my conditioned mind thinks.

We have a marital vow that says, "We promise to go on living and loving with all our hearts after the other of us has passed on." The only way for me to keep that promise is to accept, forgive, love us both, and offer to the Universe my fears for the future.

My personal progress now is that through all the years of healing, I no longer dread David's death or my own, I have a feeling that I will know how to meet our deaths with mercy and strength. Forgiveness has taken me away from dread and into the arms of inner peace. My capacity to experience my emptiness and the full range of my emotions is opening a space within where tenderness is flourishing,

That does not mean that if David dies first, I won't grieve deeply, but I know I can be there with him all the way through as he heads for the other side. I *know* I will do my own healing work and that all my *love dog* friends will support me.

I also know that if I die first, I will spend much of my time in my simple prayer to forgive the thought that I am separate from God. I believe I will find God within my dying process. As Rabia so beautifully states, "Death is the bridge whereby the lover meets the beloved."

In the past, when I was away from either Grace or Joli (my sweet animal companions) I pined for them. I see now I was projecting my separation anxiety on to them. I felt that they could not handle my being away and then I put that set of beliefs on them. I set both dogs up for missing me.

> **How can you get to that place of knowing you are never alone? One step of courageous loving-kindness at a time, you can change your experience of life. It takes work, but it is well worth it.**

Another place of profound progress for me is that while I'm in Taos for the weekend and away from Rosie, I am not pining for her and I am not assuming she is longing for me. When I think of her, I just remember she is connected with Source and she is loved beyond her wildest dreams. Our house sitter, Mary, loves Rosie and will make sure she is cared for.

Separation Anxiety

I just found out about a week ago that one of my nephews is in jail. I first spent a few days feeling helpless and wondering how I could "save" him. Now, I am simply remembering the part of me that is just like him. Each night before we go to sleep, both David and I forgive ourselves for the things we see in my sweet nephew. So, we say,

I'm so sorry, Patricia and David, for all the times you thought your mother had nothing to offer because YOU knew best. I'm so sorry, David and Patricia, for all the times in your younger years where you drank and drove; just didn't get caught. I am so very sorry for the parts of you that don't accept the need for help. I am sorry for your belligerence. I am so sorry for the part of you that feels so badly that he/she wants to kill himself/herself. I am so sorry for the parts of you that had completely given up on life. I love you. I love you. I love you right in the midst of your heartbreaking humanity.

This shifts me from feeling helpless in the face of my nephew's jail time, to feeling present and to realizing that the part of me that is him, is also in jail. I know this sounds difficult, but my internal experience is that it's very freeing. Once I see that he and I are still *One*, I can also ask the Universe to bring healing to this situation in my family and in me.

It is also so very helpful for me to remember that I am and he is also a redwood tree whether he knows it or not at this point of his journey. I don't have to save him. It's his life that he gets to live as he chooses.

When I send my nephew a card later today I will remind him that I love him dearly and deeply, irrespective of his current situation, and that I will love him all the days of his life and beyond.

The last thing I want to say is that I no longer fear those times in the future, that are sure to come, when I will experience more feelings of separation anxiety. I don't fear the fear of being alone arising once again. In fact, I almost look forward to more sessions of clearing. For me, making myself a clear channel, so that the Divine can show up and do Service through me is the only thing I am really doing here. I'm happy if separation anxiety is completely cleared or if it shows up for redemption five times today. Either way, I place myself in the hands of the *Ones I Hold Most Dear**** and I pray that all the *love dogs* reading this would know that they, too, are resting in the arms of a loving and tender God.

How can you get to that place of knowing you are never alone? One step of courageous loving-kindness at a time, you can change your experience of life. It takes work, but it is well worth it.

Our fear of being alone, the depths of our separation anxiety, is not the best place from which to make decisions. The one inside that we want to make our decisions is our most clearly connected and empowered adult (see the next soul note, "The Vehicle of Self-Compassion"). As we deal with our separation from self and God, we can learn to make decisions from a more deeply inspired place within us.

Remember that healing separation anxiety, or any other core emotional issue, requires:

- conscious awareness of the issue (we can't heal what we don't feel)
- willingness to feel the feelings surrounding the issue
- willingness to forgive ourselves
- the intention to be in the process of healing throughout our lifetime.

Another of my favorite Rumi quotes encourages us to return to ourselves again and again:

*** *The Ones I Hold Most Dear* represent all aspects of my Higher Power. In my inner world my holy ones include Rumi, Hafiz, Christ, Buddha, Papaji, St. Francis and Kabir. My holy ones also include both my beloved dogs Grace and Joli who have passed on and I feel now operate as my invisible, eternal Service dogs.

> Come, come, whoever you are,
> wanderer, worshipper, lover of leaving.
> It doesn't matter.
> Ours is not a caravan of despair.
> Come even though you have broken your vow a thousand times.
> Come, come yet again, come.
>
> (Barks, The Illuminated Rumi. Reprinted with permission.)

In closing, I'd like to ask all of the *love dogs* reading this section to pause for a moment. Let's use *Ho'oponopono* as a way of stimulating our own healing process.

Imagine you are looking in the mirror at your own beautiful self right this very moment. Imagine that you are feeling tender towards me and Rosie, Shelly, David, Celia, and Greg. Notice that you can relate to parts of all of our stories. Notice that you know there are places in you equally afraid of being alone.

Now, let's say to your own image in the mirror:

Ho'oponopono, sweet one,
I love you.
I'm so sorry for every fear you have ever had of being alone.
Ho'oponopono,
I'm sorry.
I love you.
Please, forgive me.
I'm offering all of my separation anxiety to the Universe for healing.
Ho'oponopono, sweet woman (or man),
I am so sorry that you had the losses you had in your past.
I am so sorry and I love you.

Becoming a Love Dog

Thank you for calling this to my attention for healing.
Ho'oponopono to all the ones in the world this moment who are suffering and afraid of being alone.
Ho'oponopono,
I'm sorry.
I love you, soul to soul.
Please forgive me.
Ho'oponopono.

We stand together with the hundreds and thousands of souls using the *Ho'oponopono* prayer right now for transformation and healing. We join the circle of the *Ho'oponopono love dogs*.

Let's also pause for a few moments and see yourself as a redwood tree inside a grove of beautiful redwoods. Remind yourself that your roots are deeply engaged in Mother Earth, that you have a profound connection with Source (as you define Source to be), that you have your own resources, your own humanity and divinity, and your own connection with Father Sky. Imagine feeling crisp, clean and clear, and able to let go of the emotional problems of those around you; doing only your work, the work that you came to do, and having deep compassion for the *love dogs* around you; letting them do the work they came to do.

Our collaborative intention is to honor, love, and heal separation anxiety! (Not in one fell swoop, not like a sprint but a marathon). Let's address the fear of being alone as if it's a beloved friend we are welcoming home. Amen!

Separation Anxiety

I Saw You Dancing

I saw you dancing last night on the roof
Of your house all alone.

I felt your heart longing for the
Friend.

I saw you whirling
Beneath the soft bright rose
That hung from an invisible stem in
The sky,

So I began to change into my best clothes
In hopes of joining you

Even though
I live a thousand miles away.

And if
You had spun like an immaculate sphere
Just two more times,

Then bowed again so sweetly to
The east,

You would have found God and me
Standing so near
And lifting you into our
Arms.

I saw you dancing last night near the roof
Of this world.

Hafiz feels your soul in mine
Calling for our
Beloved

—Hafiz—

(Ladinsky, *The Subject Tonight is Love - 60 Wild and Sweet Poems.* Reprinted with permission.)

The Guest House

This being human is a guest house.
Every morning a new arrival.

A joy, a depression, a meanness,
some momentary awareness comes
as an unexpected visitor.

Welcome and entertain them all!
Even if they're a crowd of sorrows,
who violently sweep your house
empty of its furniture,
still, treat each guest honorably.
He may be clearing you out
for some new delight.

The dark thought, the shame, the malice,
meet them at the door laughing,
and invite them in.

Be grateful for whoever comes,
because each has been sent
as a guide from beyond.

—Rumi—

(Barks, *The Essential Rumi*. Reprinted with permission)

The Vehicle of Self Compassion

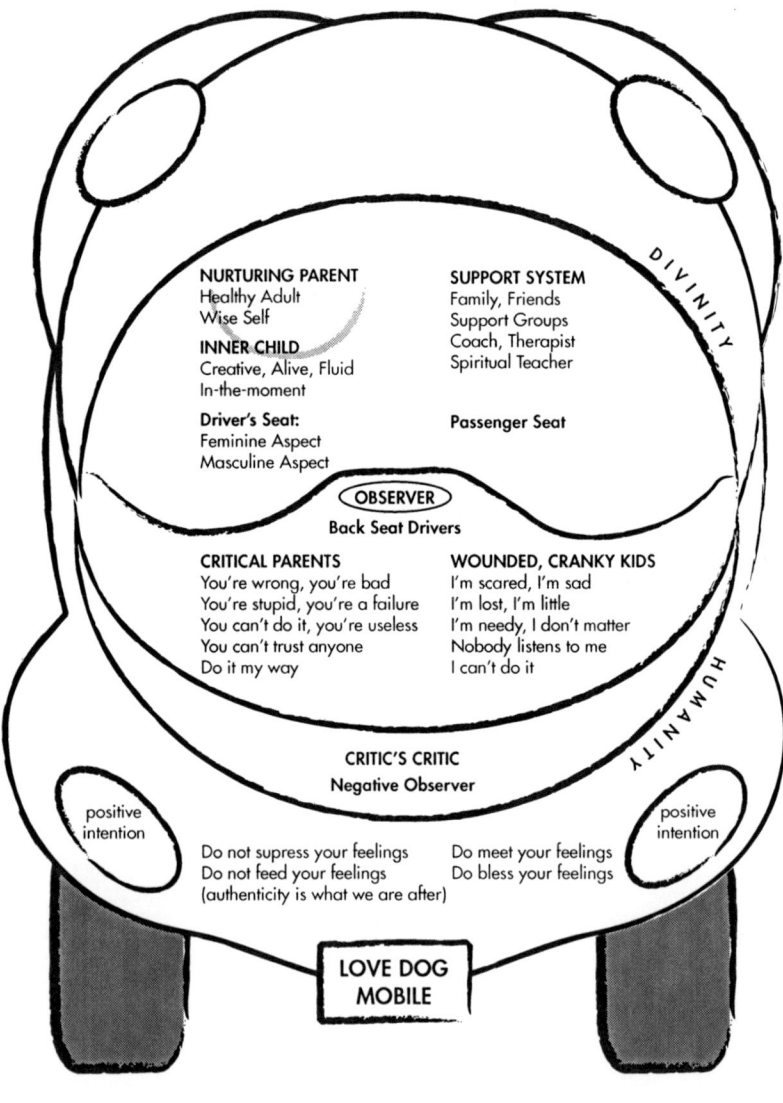

The Vehicle of Self-Compassion

Think of the countless times you feel "stuck." Perhaps you find yourself being defensive, angry, behaving in ways that you are ashamed of. Think of the times in a given day when you don't know how to communicate clearly or you don't know how to get in touch with what's happening within you. As a result, your communication and relating with others is off balance. Think of the times that you are having a landslide of emotions and you just can't accept yourself. We tend to think the problem is the landslide of emotions, when in reality the true problem is the rejection of the feelings. We do not accept our own humanity, and in that lack of acceptance, we throw ourselves out of our own hearts. We forget our own *love dog* essence.

Another way to describe this is that it's as if we are going to a building site to build ourselves a new home. Then we arrive at the site, we look in the tool kit and find we have no tools. And, furthermore, we don't have a blueprint in the toolbox. What happens next, in terms of building the building? There will be chaos, at best, *or* else the new home just won't get built.

Take a look at the car diagram on page 54. It is an overhead (and rather rustic) view of my late model Volkswagen Bug. This

The Vehicle of Self-Compassion

Vehicle of Self-Compassion provides a blueprint for how one goes about *becoming a love dog*. It gives us a way of organizing the parts of ourselves that make up who we are. When I speak of "your vehicle" in this soul note, I am speaking of you and all the different parts of you that together make up the miracle of who you are. The car provides a metaphor to understand what's happening inside our own consciousnesses.

The vehicle metaphor also gives us tools to live our lives differently. It gives us choices. It provides a compassionate, effective, and empowering system of self-management. It clearly depicts how we can shift our own thinking and emotional bodies from a place of unconscious incompetence (we don't know what's going on inside and we do not know what to do about it) to a place of conscious competence (we do know what is going on inside and we do know what to do about it.) This vehicle provides a road map for *becoming a love dog*.

> **Please remember that the "good guys" are not in the front seat and the "bad guys" in the back seat. Nobody gets to be wrong.**

Look first at the two terms at the far right side of the *Vehicle of Self-Compassion*. On the upper right side of the diagram is the word "divinity." My choice of the word divinity means that our front seat holds the healthiest, most vibrant part of self, and our support system. In other words, our truest voice, the voice that is connected to Source (whatever we name that to be) and the support system, which is a voice for our own highest self, are the front seat characters. If the term "divinity" doesn't really work for you or it's not a match for your value system, consider substituting the words "source of strength" for the word "divinity" at the top of the diagram. Julia Cameron (Cameron, *The Artist's Way*) suggests we call G – O – D, good orderly direction.

No matter if you are an atheist, agnostic, or practice any religious path, this system can be enormously helpful in working with your emotions and limiting beliefs in a very constructive and fluid fashion. If you are b*ecoming a Love Dog,* having a map depicting how you can shift from your human condition back towards your connection with Source, is as food is to a hungry man.

On the lower right side of the diagram is the word "humanity." Our human condition and all its voices are part of the back seat. This includes issues of low self-esteem, judgment, and survival, and the associated emotions of fear, anger, embarrassment, and so forth. *Please remember that the "good guys" are not in the front seat and the "bad guys" in the back seat. Nobody gets to be wrong.* Simply put, the front seat is our most conscious part of self and the back seat is the more unconscious part of self. One of my teachers, Shell Goldman, says that our unconscious (the back seat) holds as much data as a computer the size of Texas and ten stories high.

All of us have all parts of the vehicle operating. The human condition from the back seat is really just arising for purposes of our own healing. In other words when we are angry or sad or scared, those emotions are asking for kindness and attention. The voices from the backseat actually want to be included in our cars. Once we find room for them, they become part of a larger system of self-integration. Making our emotions wrong will only serve to make them stronger. Honoring our emotions gives them a chance to be blessed, and from that blessing they can rest.

When we can hold a special place for our strongest, clearest, most divine inner self *and* an equally powerful place for our own humanity, we start to experience a whole new level of integration. The war inside stops and peace begins in the showroom of our own hearts. We look in the mirror and see the reflection of a beautiful *love dog* gleaming back.

What we really want to do is to come to the place inside our being where this system of self-management becomes effortless,

The Vehicle of Self-Compassion

where all parts of the *Vehicle of Self-Compassion* are in excellent working condition. Many people think that what we want to do is eliminate or at least diminish our time in the back seat. It doesn't work. Our own humanity will continue to be part of our experience on earth throughout our lifetimes.

The best outcome is to come to terms with our humanity, make room for it in every way, then become skillful in our capacity to find the positive intention of the inner critic and to strengthen our conscious awareness of our Observers. A final intention is to build up and sustain an incredibly alive support system to empower our front seat characters.

Once we know, at any given moment, which part of the *Vehicle of Self-Compassion* we are sitting in, we are free both to acknowledge our place in the car and move around the car. To illustrate the front and back seat voices I will use an example of what sometimes goes on in my mind when it's time to begin a writing project. I feel frustrated by my lack of skill in organizing the book I am writing in the computer.

Back Seat

Critical Parent: "I am so mad at myself I could spit. I don't know what's the matter with me that I can't come to this writing project calmly and with ease. My technical skills *suck*."

Critic's Critic: "What the hell are you doing being so rough on yourself? It's not going to help if you are unkind to yourself. After all, you are a relatively new writer and do have a full time position. You should approach writing with greater tenderness."

Mid Vehicle

Observer: "I do notice that each time I start writing there is an upset that lasts anywhere from five minutes to a half hour. It would really be good for me to take a look at what this is all about."

Front Seat
Wise Self: "This is another opportunity to learn to be kind to myself with the technical skill level I have. I might also want to consider hiring a computer tutor or taking a college computer class each quarter."

Internal and External Support Systems: "I'm going to call Amba (part of my external support system) later today and ask if she can do some listening and then, perhaps, brainstorm about why I feel it's necessary to start writing time by being unkind to myself. I also want to spend time today in quiet meditation to notice more of what is going on for me."

This is a beginning understanding of how the front and back seats operate. Next I will describe each section in more detail:

The Front Seat
The Driver's Seat
In the driver's seat of the *Vehicle of Self-Compassion* sits our wisest, most compassionate self. Here sits the essence of the maturity we have on board to date and our purest version of the adult. The part of us that becomes a nurturing parent to ourselves resides in the front seat. The driver's side of the front seat is filled with the one that is intuitive, creative, resourceful, and whole. What we want to do over time is to learn to make all of our most significant decisions from this front seat position.

How many times in your life have you wished your birth parents were different? Do you remember thinking, "I wish my parents were like _____?" Do you remember the grief and despair you sometimes experienced when you noticed a particular inadequacy on the part of your parents? Maybe they were mean or absent or clueless in terms of role modeling ways to be both kind and clear so that today your own internalized parent has become a model of what your parents taught you.

Here's the good news. Today, starting this very moment, you

The Vehicle of Self-Compassion

can become that most tender and clear parent. You can reparent yourself and you can develop a daily practice in learning how to reparent yourself clearly and consistently. *In this context, to reparent means to actively become the parent to yourself that you have always longed for.*

Our inner nurturing parent contains both a feminine and a masculine aspect. The feminine aspect of our inner nurturing parent is the one who is kind and nourishing. She is spacious and open hearted. She is the one who is capable of really listening to you, especially in your darkest moments. She is the one who says, "Dear One, sweet child of my heart, please come sit on my lap so that I can hear your stories. I love you and I always have room in my heart for you." The feminine aspect of our inner adult is the one who listens and offers unconditional love.

Depending on your past parenting, it may be that you don't have access to this kind of feminine love because it truly was not prevalent in your home life. If that's the case, perhaps you can remember a beloved aunt, grandmother, guidance counselor, or coach who was good to you. You can practice retraining yourself by using inner language that they may have used. Growing an inner loving parent is not an event; it's an ongoing process, just like raising a real child.

The masculine aspect of our inner nurturing parent is the one who takes a stand, who sets boundaries, who makes sure the internal critic is not eating us alive by saying, "Stop, you cannot, I repeat cannot, treat me like that." The inner masculine is the one who guides the more practical development of the inner child. The inner masculine is the one that says, "Now that we've listened to your feelings and honored you, let's consider this direction. Here are some steps we can take in our own behalf." If the inner masculine does not know which steps to take to resolve the problem, he steps aside and asks for help.

When the inner nurturing feminine and inner nurturing

masculine work together as a team, our capacity to function in the world is greatly enhanced. When the inner mom and inner dad are holding hands and aligned in purpose, the younger part of ourselves has an inner home to go to where he/she will be nourished and guided. When these mature, loving, and practical parts of ourselves are in the driver's seat we act, respond, and make decisions in mature, loving, and practical ways. *Love dogs* are great drivers.

The driver's seat is also the home of the *inner child*. I have done a considerable amount of soul searching as to where the child should fit in the *Vehicle of Self-Compassion*. He/she actually fits in the front seat and in the back seat. The front seat *inner child* is the most creative, alive, fluid, and in-the-moment part of us. My little one inspires me, chooses colors, has wonderful ideas and is truly capable of living a spontaneous life. She is an asset.

You will note in the *Vehicle of Self-Compassion* that the *inner child* in her healthy aspect is sitting behind the nurturing parents in the driver's seat. A second aspect, the unhealthy, wounded *inner child* is sitting in the backseat and labeled the "WOUNDED, CRANKY KID." Her demands for my attention also become an asset as I begin to tune in to her needs, and meet them. So, the *inner child* sits in both places, and it is essential for us to notice which aspect of our inner child is playing out at any given time.

Passenger Seat: The Support System
Establishing an effective support system is one of the primary tasks of our maturation process. Some may feel they have traditional support systems: family, neighbors, church memberships, old friends, etc. For many of us, though, the more traditional support systems have fallen by the wayside as we live farther and farther away from one another. In our busy lives our communication networks become frayed at the seams and we often find ourselves feeling lost and cut off when we most need help.

The Vehicle of Self-Compassion

> For me to function as my very best self, living from my highest truth and most passionate expression, what kind of support do I need? Not, repeat, NOT, what do I need to do to 'get by'?

Creating a support system is, in fact, so important that our couples support group is writing an entire book on the topic called *Couples Supporting Couples* that we hope to publish in 2010. The book is about how to establish a sustainable system with another couple so that your marriage or long-term relationship can not only get through great difficulties, but also can begin to thrive.

It is important to note that the passenger seat support system contains both an internal and external aspect. Though this soul note will mostly discuss developing an external support system, an internal support system is just as important. An example of an internal support system from my own life is my internal "Board of Directors." This Board of Directors is composed of people that have supported and loved me deeply, inspired me, shown me great courage and passion, and so on. When I have an important decision to make or I am having a problem, I can call a meeting of my internal Board of Directors and get wonderful guidance and support from these wise internal voices.

The wonderful thing about an internal support system is it can be anything you can imagine. For example, I can include absolutely anyone I can think of: my loving grandmother who died many years ago, the Dixie Chicks, Buddha, Christ, or my internal nurturing parents, to name but a few. My Internal Board of Directors is a strong inner resource that actively encourages the development of my *love dog* nature and my movement from emptiness to tenderness.

Regarding a support system, whether internal or external, here is the question we must ask ourselves: "For me to function as my very best self, living from my highest truth and most passionate expression, what kind of support do I need? Not, repeat, *not*, what do I need to do to 'get by'? Rather, what kind of support would allow me to live a fulfilling life, operate a career that is both financially rewarding and in alignment with my values, and have optimal mental, emotional, physical, and spiritual health?"

> **It is an act of love for those close to you, both personally and professionally, to have an established support system.**

Here are some basic steps to consider taking as you develop your own support system and resources. Always remember to look for *love dogs!*

- Hire a coach, counselor, or helping professional of any kind as long as you feel that you can build trust and that you are getting value from the experience.
- Find a spiritual guide of some kind. That could be a minister, pastoral director, twelve-step sponsor, shaman, or rabbi. (If spirituality is not a place in your life that you feel drawn to enhance, you can let this possibility go.)
- Spend time in nature, especially if that is your point of sacred orientation.
- Create or join a support group of some kind—a women's group, a men's group, a twelve-step group, an Artist's Way group, a prayer or meditation group, a consciousness growth group, etc.
- Locate a massage therapist, an acupuncturist, a polarity body worker, a reiki practitioner, a rolfer, a physical therapist, a chiropractor, or any kind of support you can create for your ongoing physical wellbeing.
- Develop at least a few friendships that feel like "soul friendships," where you experience depth, mutuality, and kindness.

The Vehicle of Self-Compassion

- Consider an interest group like a book club, scrabble club, or bridge club that provides you an outlet for your interests.
- Set your priorities in terms of where you spend your time. Possibilities include:
  - Time for your self that may include retreat time. If, in your relationship with yourself, you see the need for very specific support—such as exercise or diet or learning a language— love yourself enough to find the targeted support that works for you.
  - Meaningful time with your family, friends, life partner, and animals.
  - Participation in the larger community.

Your support system should operate as a living, breathing organism that you review on a timely basis to ask yourself the questions: "What is it that I need now in my life? What would really support me now?"

Most of us have very busy lives. You may wonder how you would ever find the time to create or utilize a support system. If this is the case for you, I urge you to consider the idea that making time for self-care and support is essential for a healthy, balanced life.

It is an act of love for those close to you, both personally and professionally, to have an established support system. Because you care for yourself using your support resources, the significant people in your life have an opportunity to spend most of their time with you while you are either embracing your own humanity or coming from the front seat. What a gift! And, of course, your powers of observation are GREATLY enhanced by connecting with folks both personally and professionally who can point out your back seat and reinforce and encourage the development of your front seat. When my spouse goes to get support, it fills my own cup almost as much as it fills his.

The Back Seat

Our humanity lives in the back seat of our *Vehicle of Self-Compassion*. All the voices of the little wounded ones and the adult critical ones reside there. All the voices of our collective unconscious live there. All the voices of our habitual pain—the spells* we unconsciously live in—also reside in our back seat. Our back seat is a cacophony of grief cries. Our old pain, our fresh pain, the pain we take on from those around us, the pain we witness on the news everyday are all a part of what is happening in the background and in the backseat.

Our largest problem is not the backseat itself or the voices that arise from the backseat. Our largest problem is the fight we have with the backseat: the ways we try to suppress our tears, fears, and angers; the ways we club ourselves for our humanity. The clubbing is the problem!

I will share a personal example to explain the back seat characters and how they function.

The outside event: I have had an upset over the last few days with a very dear friend of mine who wants to change an aspect of our relationship. For years we have mostly felt very connected and in deep harmony. It's unusual for us to have a conflict and it's unusual not to be able to resolve it quickly and with great love and mutual respect.

The inside event: This is the story that is arising out of my back seat, the voices of my human condition that are rising as the conflict continues. I am hearing loudly from all three of my back seat characters, the critical parent, the wounded child, and the

---

* When we are acting from our patterns, we are in a spell or trance. A trance is like a wakeful sleep and may represent the youngest part of ourselves, or the most wounded—a part of us that may be lost in trauma or chaos. When we are in a spell, it's like an inner projector, replaying the movie of our lives that is stuck on a single, historical frame. We see and experience our current lives through the filter of that old, painful scene. When the "pause button" is pressed on that inner movie, we really do not see the larger picture and cannot, until we release the pause, even consider moving on.

The Vehicle of Self-Compassion

critic's critic. One way of understanding this system is that the critical parent gets on the back of the inner child and the external world. The critic's critic gets on the back of the critical parent.

The Wounded Cranky Child
Here's my little wounded, cranky child's perspective in this situation: "She hurt my feelings. She wants to change our friendship. She's leaving me. I'm so sad. I'm scared. She's my best friend. What would I do without her? I can't make it? I'm devastated. I can't live without her. I'm mad at her for all the things she has on her list that are more important than me. I'm going to take my marbles and go home. I can't stop crying."

> We do not want to be too indulgent with the wounded one, and we do not want to assume she is who we are today. She is a memory that we hold from the past, and she is also a part of a spell we are currently acting out from our past memories.

This is an example of the little one's catastrophic perspective. She is inconsolable at this point in time. She has interpreted this situation through the eyes of the seven-year-old whose father died in an industrial accident and whose grieving mother was no longer available emotionally.

Sometimes I forget that I am truly *not* five or seven or nine years old and I'm not a teenager and I'm not a young adult. I am actually sixty years old today. I am a fully grown and highly functioning adult. But, when I let little Patti take the wheel (and it feels as if she's living in my belly), I don't make good choices. Then, the gas that I'm using to fuel my vehicle is fear, catastrophizing, stubbornness, hurt, and anger. If you could imagine that a seven-year-old is actually driving the car, she would be running over the embankment, driving into trees, and steering the car all over the road. Part of the job of the healthy inner parent is to get the wheel away from the little kid so that the adult can drive.

The way we get the wheel away from the little one is not by yelling at her or shaming her. It's by stopping the vehicle and pausing to listen. It's by holding her awhile and being tender with her. Perhaps then she'll take a nap or be content to ride along when a more competent driver takes the wheel.

We do not want to be too indulgent with the wounded one, and we do not want to assume she is who we are today. She is a memory that we hold from the past, and she is also a part of a spell we are currently acting out from our past memories.

The Critical Parent
In the example where my friend wants to change our relationship, my critical parent, when judging the inner child, sounds like this: "Grow up, you big baby. Don't be so sensitive. How do you expect to make it in life crying like a big baby all the time? You make me sick. I'm embarrassed to be associated with you. You give us a bad name. I'm sick of it. Grow up! Get off it! It's not that big a deal. You are being way too demanding! You are making a mountain out of a molehill, yet again. Why don't you just go to your room, close the door, and not come out again? I mean it!"

When my critical parent's wrath is turned in my friend's direction, it sounds like this:

"She's wrong and she should get off of it. She's way too demanding. How dare she do this? I am pissed off! She has no right to consider changing our relationship. Who does she think she is? Who cares? I don't need her. I'm out of here. I don't have to put up with this. I'm furious. I want to get even with her. I want to leave her."

I call the approach this aspect of self is taking the "Hitlerian" approach after Adolph Hitler. It's an aspect of self that is crude, judgmental, angry, and harsh without any possibility of redemption. The basic and simple message of the critical parent is, "You suck!"

Remember—the adult and child back seat perspective are a natural part of our humanity. It's not really possible to skip the voices that arise when we are emotionally triggered. If we try to skip them, they come out sideways. We kick the cat. We stuff them. We act out because of them.

Here's another essential reminder for working with the back seat characters. If we consider them friends, not adversaries, we can attentively listen and they can communicate less loudly. Remember how it has felt for you in a time that you've been truly upset and then had the benefit of a friend who is really "there" for you. You know what it feels like to have someone listen without judgment and offer a tender response. We can offer that to ourselves and that, once again, is an example of reparenting. We remain *love dogs* because of our pure intention to return to the front seat and integrate the back seat, no matter where we are in the car.

The Critic's Critic
Now I want to move to another truly significant part of this *Vehicle of Self-Compassion:* the negative observer who sits on the bumper and hammers away at our back seat—the critic's critic. The critic's critic is the place where much of our pain truly resides.

My experience is that most of the pain I feel is not so much that I'm angry, or frightened, or sad, or having a major upset and huge potential loss. The critical parent and the cranky kid in the back seat have an honorable perspective. When I can make room for them, they become messengers. They are just voices expressing my humanity. I don't have to give them juice. I don't have to make them wrong. I don't have to fuel them with drama and panic. When I can embrace my back seat buddies, I am really okay. I actually have a sense of "coming home" to myself.

> The critic's critic is the place where much of our pain truly resides.

The critic's critic is the place within where I begin to war with myself. In the current example, the critic's critic sounds like this: "I should not have these feelings. I should be over them. I should not be in reaction. I should not be human. What is the matter with me that I am having so much emotion? I should get a grip. I should get some help. I should have no attachment and no places that are broken or wounded in me. I should have handled my family systems background entirely. I should not be in a spell. I should be conscious 100% of my time. This is ridiculous. I am a human potential teacher. What is the matter with me?" The basic and simple message of the critic's critic to the critical parent is, "You suck for thinking you suck."

The one who sits on the bumper ranting and raving about what's going on in the back seat is the one who tries to sabotage the possibility of my creating a more whole and integrated self. The one sitting on the bumper is shooting me in the foot. *And—this is very important—dealing with the critic's critic is the step that allows a whole new level of inner connection and opens the doorway to genuine transformation.*

Once I am in the place of refusing to shame my back seat, I can begin to ask myself the question, "Well, what is the positive intention of my critic's critic? What would her message be if she were more skillful and if she could come from a place of tenderness towards my process?" My kindness and *love dogness* are one.

If my critic's critic took off her boxing gloves and spoke in a clear, true voice about what it is that she wants to get my attention about, what would it be? In the example I've been using about the conflict with my friend, here is the critic's critic positive intention: "Let's pay attention here. It's obvious that so much pain is coming up that it's related to unresolved history. This is an opportunity. Let's use it to find a whole new level of self-compassion." My critic's critic really just wants me to pause, to attend to myself, to integrate, to forgive, and to move towards more conscious awareness of my inner dialogue. She is shouting at me because she wants me to have more freedom. It's very helpful when I can get her to stop with the shouting and just deliver the message.

Mastering the discovery of the positive intention of the critic's critic is a vital part of developing emotional maturity and increased self-compassion.

The Positive Observer
The Observer is the one who sits in the very center of the *Vehicle of Self-Compassion*, in the center of our own beings. The Observer is constantly aware of our position in the car. She is the one whose job it is to notice what's happening in our inner dialogue. Without the Observer, transformation is not available. If we don't notice our front seat/back seat position, we have no choices. When we are totally unconscious of our inner dialogue, that gives the back seat and the critic's critic free range to take over the front seat. We end up bullying our best self. When this occurs, we drive all over the road. We have no map in our hands and we are really out of control.

When I begin working with clients, most do not have a system of self-management that leads them to self-compassion. Most clients begin by believing they "are" their back seat and they "are" their critic's critic. They believe that their human condition is their true identity. Most clients come from a family system where their parents did not have a system of self-management so they projected their entire backseat onto the client. Now the client has internalized his or her parents' back seats. They treat themselves in a way that is familiar, based on how they were raised. Again, this is another aspect of a spell. We are in a dream based on our parent's projection of who we are, and we have not paused to self-reflect. We have not taken the time to create our own identity, or to discover who and what we *truly are:* connected with source, full of wisdom and compassion, possessing our own aspects of greatness, a nurturing parent, and learning to create a never ending love for ourselves. We may not know much about our front seat at all. And, when that is true, it's really time to invest ourselves in coming to know the voice that springs from the Great Silence. It's time to know the soul self and the one who comes from truth that lives outside any spell and is beyond our humanity.

Here's what my Observer says about this current situation stimulated by the conflict with my old friend:

"Wow, we've really gotten triggered here. We have a rule of thumb that whenever our emotions escalate past five, on a scale of one to ten, then history is involved. It's really good that we had a session yesterday with our coach to discover what's really going on. I see that we've moved considerably from our positions yesterday where we were both lost in the back seat and judging from the bumper as the critic's critic. This morning it feels more like this material needed to come up so that we can take it to another level of self-compassion. We can trust our friend to do her part of the sorting process, as we have not had any experience with her where she doesn't look at her self. We can trust ourselves to do our own work, work we have done so many thousands of times. Probably, in the long run, this conflict will make us both clearer and closer, and I look forward to seeing myself through the rest of its resolution.

I want to pause a moment and bless each of the voices from the back seat. Thank you for what you have had to say. You are welcome here. I have room in my heart for you. This conflict is not an indication that something or someone is wrong. It is an indication that both of us want something that feels more loving and truer for us now."

My last point of observation is that since my friend wants to change a part of our relationship, I will need to be sure I find another way to get my needs met. I'm a grown up here and she is my beloved friend; she's not my Source. God is my Source. Perhaps later today I can write about all the things I'm learning and I can continue to get help until our conflict is completely resolved and we are back to feeling truly mutual.

What grace it is to use my relationships as such a place of self-discovery and to have a friend who does the same. My friend and I, even in the midst of conflict, remain *love dogs*.

Many Months Later
You might be wondering the result of this process triggered by my dear friend. Because both she and I have extensive internal and external support systems, we have both grown immeasurably by working through the conflict. Our soul friendship has deepened and matured. Without our support systems, this friendship could easily have ended up in the friendship graveyard along side other lost relationships.

Her request that I stop sharing so much about my work, which initially freaked me out, has now become a deeply abiding healing for me. I can see, looking back, that I was absolutely too lost in work and clients. Now I've asked my life coach to support me with clients and that is much easier and more efficient. My friend's willingness to challenge me and be a tuning fork in my life has been wonderful. I now have much better boundaries in both my personal and professional lives.

Moving Around the Vehicle of Self-Compassion
Movement begins, in part, just by beginning to notice that we have a sense of internal voices. When we can pinpoint where we are in the car in a given moment, we have taken a wonderful step because we have turned on the light of the positive Observer.

If, when we pause, we hear that a much younger, littler voice is speaking, we can always stop to heart listen: "Little One, did I hear you say…" Many times the act of our healthy adult listening to the wounded child, in and of itself, is enough to soothe the child so she can relax.

Sometimes the wounded child needs to be redirected or reeducated by the front seat characters. They might say: "These are the steps we will take…" "Here is how we intend to take care of you…" or "This is our adult decision…"

How do we turn to the nurturing parent in the front seat and access that caring voice within? It might be as simple as inwardly inviting the nurturing parent to step forward. Another good technique is to change physical positions. We might say, "That chair belongs to the nurturing parent. When I sit there I intend for the nurturing parent to contribute its wisdom and love!"

If you have trouble accessing the nurturing parent, imagine what a loving figure in your life might say to the wounded child. If your own parents don't fit the bill, think of someone who does. This might be a grandparent, a dear friend, or a supportive teacher.

We can access any of the front seat passengers in our vehicles in just this same way. It is always helpful to pause and check in with the Observer and see what is going on with all the passengers. That will give us a chance to take a breath and get some perspective. Then we might say, "This feels way too serious. Let's hear from the playful, joyous inner child." Or we might call a meeting of our internal Board of Directors to hear the wisdom of the absolutely unlimited resources we have within.

Encourage a dialogue between the passengers. After the internal nurturing parent has comforted the inner child, for example, it's often helpful to move back to the inner child to see how the parent's tender language has landed. There will probably be related fears and concerns that the nurturing parent can address.

Many of us have times full of negative thinking, heavy criticism, and painful emotions. Again, if we can begin by listening

The Vehicle of Self-Compassion

without judgment, that in itself will often ease the pain. If the criticism is directed toward a young inner voice, or the people and situations in our lives, it's the critical parent that's taken over.

When the critical parent is hammering the wounded child, we can often access the nurturing parent and have them take a stand for that young part. They can say something like: "I hear your pain, rage, upset, and judgments. I'll give you a brief window of time to vent. Take ten minutes to write it out or to call a friend and speak it out. When the ten-minute window is over, it's time to shift towards being kind to ourselves."

This is not always easy and depending on the level of pain you are in, and the amount of history that is triggered, you may need to get help from your support system to make the shift.

Sometimes it is helpful to discover the positive intention behind the back seat voice. The critical parent might say, for example, "I only want the inner child to be able to cope with the challenges of the world." This would be a specific positive intention. The nurturing parent might respond, "Great! I want that as well. Tell me, does it look to you like browbeating this young part of us is accomplishing our goal? From my perspective it is just making the situation much worse. It's time for some support, love, and understanding."

Remember that any confusion about which voice we are in and the inability to shift our voices are part of the journey. We want to be as tender with ourselves as we can while we are deepening with this model. As we practice we will gain skill and understanding.

It is very helpful to talk out loud or write in a journal as we move around the *Vehicle of Self-Compassion*. This helps ground the experience and makes it more real. Having a trusted friend silently witness our explorations lends power, focus, and acceptance as we give airtime to the different internal voices.

I find the ecstatic poetry of Rumi, Hafiz, Lalla, David Whyte, and Mary Oliver supports me both in integrating my back seat and reconnecting with my front seat. These poets are *love dog* mentors.

All of us can use support in deepening the process of reparenting. We might attend a workshop such as those offered by Leading From the Heart** to deepen our understanding. Hiring a therapist or coach can be a great help as we build relationships with our inner voices and learn more about the unconscious mind.

Following is a poem I wrote about finding and naming my own inner parent.

TENDERNESS IS MY TRUE PARENT

I lost my parents when I was very, very young.
One to death and the other to
the emotional havoc the death stimulated.
I have been searching for them everywhere.

I've been looking into the eyes of every teacher,
therapist, coach, counselor, minister, friend, or lover
to find that one who will never leave me.

I've been bringing my pining song
to workshops, trainings, seminars, and retreats
all across the United States, FOREVER!

All honor to my soul in this search.

** Go to www.becomingalovedog.com for a schedule of Leading From the Heart's upcoming workshops.

The Vehicle of Self-Compassion

Then, very late one night,
sleepless, bereft, and weeping the tears of abandonment,
I found the one I was looking for.
Her name is Tenderness and she lives deep inside
of me in a place called Grace.
She is my true parent
She is my only parent
She is the one who will always, always kiss me on the forehead.
She is the one who has room for my entire emotional range.
She is the one I hold most dear,
and, she is always, always, here.

With the night sky as my cradle and the slivered moon as my witness,
I say a sweet prayer for my own dear heart
and all the ones everywhere feeling abandoned and alone this
very moment in time.

—Patricia Flasch—

Becoming a Love Dog

What if We Cannot Move Around the Vehicle?
There are times we really can't move around the car—when the movement within the vehicle is stalled. What then? I'll share an example from my own life.

> And, I want to tell you, *love dog* friend, that even in the times when you, too, feel absolutely powerless to shift, you are still inherently lovable.

I was in the midst of editing an article and I was really getting nowhere. I could see the problem with the article. I could see what didn't work. But I was clueless as to how to sort it out. Then, in making an attempt to rewrite, I accidentally deleted five paragraphs that had just taken me more than an hour to write. I was furious.

I had been up in the mountains sitting by a stream using my laptop. I just could not get movement to occur on the writing project or within myself. I stewed all the way home. I stewed for a few more hours at home. I could see that I was hearing from both the critical parent and the critic's critic. While I could observe where I was positioned in the vehicle clearly, I was really helpless to do anything whatsoever about it. I could not shift.

Since I could not shift, I spent my time internally ripping myself to shreds because I COULD NOT SHIFT. This served to deepen my angst considerably.

One of the other projects I was going to work on at the time was, "Moving around the *Vehicle of Self-Compassion.*" How could I possibly write about that when I myself was frozen in place? Then it occurred to me, "Well, sweetheart, maybe readers want to know what to do when you can't shift." Maybe this "not moving around the car" also has value.

I want to offer myself compassion for those painful hours. I just couldn't do it any other way at that moment in time. While this morning I do have some perspective, I do also want to pay

The Vehicle of Self-Compassion

tribute to the lost hours. And, I want to tell you, *love dog friend*, that even in the times when you, too, feel absolutely powerless to shift, you are still inherently lovable. When the inside of your *Vehicle of Self-Compassion* is stalled, the best possible thing to do is **nothing**. The best possible approach to take when you cannot make an inner shift is to pause, notice you cannot shift, and love yourself right there, right in the middle of your own heartbreaking humanity. There have been times in my life when I have been unable to shift on a particular issue for days, weeks, months, and on occasion, years.

Early this morning, though, when I was able to return to a place of tenderness for myself, I could see that the lost hours truly did have value. I could also make a conscious decision that if the only way to meet my goal of having the web page soul notes done by July 31st is to push myself mercilessly, then the timing of the goal needs to shift. Being kind to myself is definitely more important to me in the larger picture, and in this very moment, more important to me than any goal or particular outcome.

By giving up on the idea that I could shift—that I could move around the vehicle—and accepting myself in the midst of my own turmoil, I could once again, begin to shift perspective. This is called *surrender*. Once we surrender, new life and a new way of looking at things is born. We become *love dogs*.

Final Thoughts on Self-Management
This model of the *Vehicle of Self-Compassion* is always a work in progress. I've been using this system with my clients and myself for almost two decades. But it changes because it is alive and it grows with my own evolution. It is a fluid rather than a static model. Just as Detroit has new automobile models each year, with refinements and improvements, this system of self-management is evolving too. This is the 2009 model.

Becoming a Love Dog

> My prayer is that this system of self-management will help you deepen your relationship with your true self beyond your wildest dreams.

It is fine for each of us to question the model as we use it, and to sort out our own answers inside our own beings. Whatever framework of understanding we end up with, noticing the unconscious and how it plays an active role in our life and experience is a tremendous step of progress.

The purpose of this model is not to know exactly where we are in the car every single moment. We don't have to check the "right" seat in the car diagram each time we turn our attention inward. The *Vehicle of Self-Compassion* is a guide. Its purpose is to help make sense of our internal dialogue. The most important part of understanding is that we come to know we have a back seat and a front seat, or an unconscious and conscious mind. Even if we can't decipher where we are in the back seat, that we know there is a back seat is significant.

This model has changed my internal experience and the inner experiences of my clients and students hundreds of thousands of times. It takes willingness and stamina to become truly skillful with this model of *becoming a love dog*. And it takes a great deal of self-forgiveness during the times we don't know where we are in the car and we don't know how to shift gears.

Thank you, dear reader, for listening. I offer this piece of work to anyone who would like to deepen their contact with their own soul by having this process become a part of their path. If you discover new aspects of how it works in your own life, we'd love to hear from you.

My prayer is that this system of self-management will help you deepen your relationship with your true self beyond your wildest dreams. I pray that you recognize and deepen your *love dog* nature.

The Vehicle of Self-Compassion

In closing this soul note, I wanted to end with some powerful words offered by my own inner wise woman/most nurturing parent. This is a letter she writes to all the wounded ones inside of me. I share it in hopes that it will encourage you to increase your capacity to be tender with yourself, to open to that deeply loving part of yourself, irrespective of what is going on in your life or in the midst of your human condition. We so often seek answers outside ourselves, while the deeper truth is that we are looking for self-soothing; for a kind of deep kindness towards ourselves from within ourselves so that we can rest in the arms of a loving God or Goddess that lives inside.

Dear Sweet Woman of My Heart:

I want you to know how very much I love you. I love you as big as the mountain and as deep as the sea. I love you with a never-ending love. I love you with my whole heart and in every cell of my being.

Know that while you grieve for the loss of your sweet old dog, I am here loving you. Whether you are lonely or sad or completely disconnected from the heart of your grief, I love you.

I love you when you use food and while you are using food to try to suppress this great emptiness. I love you when you think the refrigerator has your answer and I love you in the times when you remember that you can be present with this great void. I love you when you try to medicate your grief with food or television or romance novels. I truly love you. This now moment, I love you.

I love you when this current loss brings up all the other old losses. I love you when you are stumbling over in grief and when you cannot stop weeping. I love you when your grief has subsided.

I love you for the hundreds of thousands of times in the past when you have been grieving and could not comfort yourself. I love you in the times that you have used medicine to see yourself through the grief and I love you for the times when you have not chosen medicine as an antidote for grief.

My love for you knows no bounds.

Becoming a Love Dog

I will love you if this grief lasts for days and weeks and months. I will love you if this grief continues throughout your whole lifetime. I will love you all the days of your life and even after you die.

I have been HERE in all your darkest moments, even when it has seemed to you that you are lost or disconnected from me, your internal wise woman. I have always been here in the great silence loving you. When you cannot hear me, please know that I am still here, an invisible eternal presence that never ever leaves you.

With love and tenderness,
Patricia

> This above all: to thine own self be true.
>
> —William Shakespeare—

Developing Inner Authority

From our earliest memories, we are taught to respect authority. This early authority is made up of our parents, older siblings, our religious structures, educational institutions, governmental agencies, and so on. Our very survival at the onset of our lives may depend on our capacity to respect authority (or at least obey authority.)

> Individuation, giving birth to our essential selves, is an elemental and necessary ingredient in creating and sustaining a long term loving relationship with ourselves and the Divine.

As we age, looking for answers outside of ourselves rather than inside of us can cause significant problems. It's as if what we needed when we were young to survive now teaches us not to question authority. When we are unable to question authority, as adults, then we must live the lives we are told to live, not the lives we want to live. This prevents us from thriving and living in an integrated internal and external world.

Developing Inner Authority

When we know our own voices and can speak our truth to anyone at any time, we are operating as fully functioning adults. When our inside world matches our actions, then our external world reflects an internally integrated world. We are who we say we are and we behave that way.

Today, when questioning authority is so needed in our family systems, in our culture, and in our larger world, we are in a spell. We have been following leaders who often do not have our best interests at heart. We are taught that to question the war is to commit treason. Yet, to not question the war is unconscionable and is, in fact, why so many of our former allies are wondering what is going on with America. We have either stopped listening to our inner voice, we've given up, or we are so enraged we are unable to act in our own behalf. This saddens me.

To have *inner authority* means that we have taken ultimate responsibility for our own lives. We know we are the captains of our own ships. We have authorship for our own path in every sense of the word. When we are living from our inner authority, we make decisions by listening clearly to our intuition; our wisest and most compassionate self.

Often we grow up to be fine upstanding citizens, respecting the outer authority meticulously, *or* we rebel and go to the other end of the spectrum. Either way, if we follow in our parents' footsteps *without question* or if we rebel, we have not gone through the appropriate developmental process to find our own inner authority.

When we have not matured to the point of developing, discovering, and acting on our own inner authority, we have an over dependence on authority figures. We often have a hard time making decisions, or we hire so many experts that we can't hear our own voice. We give our power to individuals claiming to have the answers.

We might ask, "What does a chapter on inner authority have

to do with the central theme of this book, *Becoming a Love Dog*? I believe that individuation, giving birth to our essential selves, is an elemental and necessary ingredient in creating and sustaining a long term loving relationship with ourselves and the Divine.

If we don't have a clear sense of self, we are not going to be able to have a clear sense of a relationship and it will be difficult to connect with the Divine. If we are not operating from a position of inner emotional maturity, we will not be able to have emotionally mature relationships with others.

If we have not done the inner work to individuate from our parents, our spouses often become our parents. We begin to play out the same games that we played as children and feel powerless within our relationships. To the extent that we are internally living as if we are part of our birth families and behave in childish ways in response to our partners, we are actively participating in the breakdown of our primary relationships. This breakdown happens when we react to our life partners as if they are our parents or siblings (or our children or ex-spouses.) Then we are not in our best adult selves nor are we allowing our partner their full adult status, and our relationships suffer accordingly. Rather than *love dog* meeting *love dog*, we are caught in a power struggle with critical parents and inner kids.

If we rebelled against our parents, we tend to act out of rebellion in our partnerships. We continue to test our partner and push the limits. If our partner has a valid request we tend to project that they are trying to control us and we refuse to acknowledge the request. Indications that we have unaddressed authority issues are lots of power struggles in our relationships, relationships based on hierarchical standards rather than equality or mutuality, and playing the "one up/one down" game.

This is not a black/white issue. All of us have, to some extent, individuated and all of us have places where we are stuck in old family patterns.

Developing Inner Authority

The key is to start where we are. A great beginning is to see clearly the ways that we are operating as a grown up, whole self *and* to observe the ways that we are regressed, responding to our partner as if they are our parent.

As an example, let's say that your life partner comes home one evening and lets you know he would like to attend a four-day men's retreat in Colorado Rocky Mountains. Let's also assume that your world is in relative order—the kids can be covered, the mortgage is paid, and you feel it is equally conceivable that you could take time to go to a writing workshop or women's retreat.

A response from a place of emotional maturity might go as follows: You encourage your partner to attend the retreat, with your blessings, and hope he has a wonderful weekend. You let your partner know you'll miss him *and* that you are looking forward to some time with yourself and to pursue your own interests. You are happy to offer your partner "roots and wings." In other words, you let him know that you will be glad for his return *and* that you really support his going away and having time for himself. You *know* that you will be *okay* without him and his personal freedom is important to you. You have a deep respect for your own individual freedom so it's easy to offer that same gift to him.

If you have some early abandonment issues that are unresolved from your family of origin, you are more likely to REACT to his possible departure. You are more likely to think that his going away is about *you*, rather than an expression of his interests and an encouragement of his aliveness and self-care. You are more likely to regress and behave as if your partner today is the daddy who divorced your mom and left you when you were very little. When you are unconsciously regressed, you do not realize that your early and unresolved wounding is having a dramatic effect on your current relationship. Your *love dog* nature has been overrun by past history.

When you are operating from a place of emotional maturity,

and you are the male partner going to the seminar, you would be delighted to have found a wonderful retreat to attend and would look forward to the rest, fun, and personal growth. You would make arrangements for your responsibilities at home to be covered while you are away. You would also care for your partner in terms of letting her know you love, honor, and appreciate her. You might offer to have a date prior to your departure or on your return so that she knows how deeply you value her. This can assist her in more easily supporting your private journey. You look forward to the time away from relationship *and* you look forward to sustaining your connection with your partner, and the *love dog connection* remains.

Alternatively, responding from a place of inner authority means that you can deal with any internal issues that arise in this situation because you have developed relationship skills like reparenting, non-violent communication, or work with a relationship counselor or coach.

> **Rather than continuing to feed (and perhaps even shout) our polarized positions and insist that our point of view is the "right" view, we pause to soften our tone and to begin to listen deeply to one another.**

If you are operating from a place of old conditioning and core wounding you are more likely to deliver your message from defensiveness. You are more likely to insist your partner support your weekend away. You are more likely to see going to the weekend as a way to rebel, much as you once did in your family of origin. If you are in that age-old pain of your mother's smothering, you are more likely to use the weekend as an opportunity to ACT OUT that old story. You are more likely to overlay your partner with your mother and let her have the full measure of your old rage at your controlling mother.

It's also possible that you could be at a place where you are integrating your core pain and that would allow you to be in complete integrity with your partner, as well as yourself. In other words, if your partner's leaving for a four-day weekend does bring up old abandonment issues, you can tell the truth about that. You can say, "My little one has just returned to the place where 'daddy's leaving' and I know that's not about our current partnership."

You could ask for reassurance. You could remind your partner that even though your little one needs attention you do still very much support their time for themselves and their weekend journey. You would let your partner know that you are capable of reparenting your own little one *and* that you appreciate this opportunity to come to know yourself better.

If you are the partner leaving for the weekend and you notice that you have begun REACTING to your partner's less than enthusiastic response, you can also tell your truth about that as soon as you notice it. That might sound something like this: "Whew, I notice I've just started going back to that place where Mom calls the shots and I'm pissed off. I do know that's not so much about you and me, in this present moment, as it is about my unresolved pain with my mom. So, let me just take a moment to be with my little one."

If you are able to let your partner go with ease, or you are able to be honest about your own internal process without projecting it on your partner, you are in a place of emotional maturity. Your individuation work is well underway. Your connection as *love dogs* is growing. If not, there is more work to be done.

An example that I often like to use when teaching relationship seminars with my husband, David, is this: imagine that we are standing looking towards the audience, at times in our marriage we are standing close together, arm in arm, facing life as a team. There are other times we are standing further apart with just the tips of our fingers touching as we go forward in life. Sometimes we are not touching. Each is completely engaged in his or her individual journey. Still, in those times, our hearts are aligned *and* we are deeply engaged in our individual experience of roots and wings.

In our marriage we often affirm together, "In our home and in our hearts, partnership rules." What that means is that rather than continuing to feed (and perhaps even shout) our polarized positions and insist that our point of view is the "right" view, we pause to soften our tone and to begin to listen deeply to one another. We really look to see if we can find the strength in one another's position and the greater truth. Listening to our own and one another's inner authority is a rich way to live.

I would like to briefly expand this discussion beyond primary relationships. When we do not have well developed inner authority in the business arena, we often invest in unequal partnerships—the one up/one down dynamic. We project onto our business partners the unresolved issues we have with our parents. We don't see how we can speak our mind or take our stand and still be equal partners. We give our partner too much power, and then resent them for taking it. Or we can take the lion's share of power and become the parent, resenting the lack of support from the partner we have put in the one down position.

We know we have developed inner authority when we have a clear sense of who we are, what we want, and when we can create and sustain a clear focus. We are well on our way to operating from inner authority when someone disagrees with us and we can listen objectively, without defensiveness, and are open to cooperation without losing touch with our own inner knowing.

Partnership is the path out of power struggles. In partnership we meet at the table as equals and *love dogs*. No one is up and no one is down. We know we have equal value. We experience a sense of mutuality, of being met at the table. There is a feeling that the sum of our parts equals a much greater whole.

Developing Inner Authority

Inner Authority Assessment – Steps Toward Individuation
Here is a process to assess the degree to which you are coming from inner authority in different areas of your life:

Make four columns on a piece of paper. Title the columns as follows:
- External Beliefs and Values (from authority figures, parents, grandparents, etc.)
- My Questioning (of those beliefs and values)
- My Rebellion (against those beliefs and values)
- My inner authority (my own considered position)

The idea here is to notice whether or not we have integrated the beliefs and values of our authority figures without question, or whether we have really sorted our initial value system to see what feels true to us today. Ultimately what we want is to examine our early values and then make new choices, where appropriate, in alignment with our own values.

Take different sets of beliefs and values from authority figures in your life and put them in the first column. Then examine how you have dealt with those beliefs and values in your own life in columns two and three. In column four, name your own beliefs and values: "This is who I am within my core values today."

Here is an example of my own inner authority assessment:

1. External Beliefs and Values: My paternal grandparents taught me Catholic values. My grandparents were very religious and prayed the rosary every single day of their fifty-three-year marriage including the day their beloved son, Jim, my father, died a tragic and accidental death. The Catholic Mass was both their religious and spiritual center and a large part of their social network. (My grandparents adored me and I equally adored them.)

2. My Questioning: I began questioning the Catholic doctrine at age nineteen. I didn't believe that the priest had the right to say that women choosing abortion were going to hell. I didn't believe that priests were the go-between for my relationship with God. I believed that I could go directly to God inside myself and that I had my own profound access to Source. I did not believe the pope was infallible.

3. My Rebellion: I rebelled and left the Catholic Church at the same time my first marriage ended. I was both ashamed of walking away and knew it was right for me. I left the Church because I didn't agree with some of the doctrine and because the Church was no longer a place of sanctuary. My questions were not welcome. I became what the Church considers a "lapsed" or "fallen away" Catholic. This was the conscious aspect of my rebellion: I was absolutely clear about the choice I was making and the reasons behind it.

   The unconscious part of my rebellion was that I had no idea that this "stand" was also about my familial history and need to strike out on my own. While I knew I was walking away from my religious upbringing, I did not know that I was also maturing and becoming my own person. I was becoming a risen Catholic, not a lapsed Catholic.

4. My inner authority: As I continued my own spiritual journey, I was able to sort out the difference between form (religion) and essence (Spirit). While I never returned to the Catholic Church, I have an incredibly eclectic spiritual path. What I have chosen to "keep" from my grandparents' values was their "true devotion." I now believe that my grandparents modeled a life that was a "prayer without ceasing," and I strive for the same level of devotion on

my spiritual path. I believe that my grandparents would be pleased with the living ministry that I offer through my work today as a Soul Whisperer. Both my grandparents were, and are, *love dogs*. The form they chose was different, the essence the same.

An essential part of our spiritual and emotional maturity has to do with sorting out the beliefs and values that we truly do want to keep from the past, renaming and reclaiming those values in our own lives, and releasing the parts of our parental and historical background that no longer serve us today.

One extremely important piece that I've kept from the Catholic tradition is "centering prayer." Father Thomas Keating inspired the use of this prayer as a way for Catholics and those of any faith to come together around the center of a holy, self-chosen word. For example, my practice of "centering prayer" is to take twenty minutes every day to sit in the quiet of my own heart and focus on my word, "tenderness." I have a soul friend and spiritual director, Susan Rush, who guides me in my fidelity to the prayer and who helps me take my practice deeper.

What we are really talking about here is coming to emotional and spiritual maturity. If you have not yet given yourself permission to look towards your inner authority, now is the time. If you are 20 or 30-40-50-60-70 or 80 years old, take a stand, right now, that you have the birthright to complete your own individuation, that you are unique, creative, resourceful and whole. The truth is: "*It is completely okay and safe for me to grow up. I have my own path, my own inner authority.*" To individuate means to have become your own whole and integrated human being.

---

* To find out more about Susan Rush and her contemplative prayer retreats, go to www.centeringnm.com

The Cost of Not Following our Inner Authority

There is always a cost to not following inner authority. A clear example occurred years ago when I was taking a yoga class. The instructor, whom I highly regarded, suggested the class do a handstand. I said I didn't think my arms were strong enough. The teacher said, "You don't know your strength until you do the posture." I replied, "I really don't think my forearms are strong enough. I don't feel sure of myself." The teacher said. "Trust me on this one. Go for it!" I said a third time, "I don't think this is a good idea," and again the teacher said I could do it. I then attempted the handstand and fell on my head. I spent the next six months getting chiropractic treatments, instead of doing yoga. In this case there was a huge cost to pay when I revered the teacher's authority and denied my own voice. There is always a cost. It may be as simple and as damaging as living someone else's life instead of your own.

It is easy in our society to allow outer authority figures to make our decisions for us. It certainly takes less effort to just accept the opinions and directions of politicians, for example, that we have made into father figures or doctors we have made into gods. Recognizing our inner authority means taking responsibility for our bodies, our government and our lives in cooperation with medical experts, political figures, and those close to us. History is riddled with tragedies that follow from societies blindly following outer authority.

Another example of not following inner authority occurred when I was writing a book of new thought prayers a few years ago and took the compilation of prayers to an editor. One of the first comments the editor made was that words like Peace, Inner Space, and Emptiness—words I think of as a part of God—should not be capitalized. I took the information, invalidated my own belief system, and put the book and my writing away. This unconscious response to the editor was a prime example of a lack of inner authority. The cost is that the book remains in my desk drawer. Of course, I can choose to resurrect it any moment as a stand for my inner authority.

In order to return to my writing, I had to revisit that situation and realize that I gave up my own power and direction. I then needed to decide clearly, within my own truth, whether those words should be capitalized or not. What I chose doesn't matter. That I chose from my inner authority makes all the difference.

We have all spent years not following our inner authority. There is no point in shaming ourselves about this. Rather, let's use the memory of the price we paid as our fuel to make the choice of taking a step of courage and following our inner authority.

Trusting and acting on our own inner authority is often difficult. It helps to drop out of our heads and into our bodies, our gut, and take the step of courage. It helps to break a big task down into small steps and take a step in allegiance with our inner authority.

Following our Inner Authority
Following our inner authority is often a step of courage. The voice of inner authority will often be at odds with what we were taught and what those around us are telling us to do. Inner authority and *inner integrity* go hand in hand.

Several years ago, my friend and fellow *love dog*, Amba, received a mammogram that showed that she had calcification in her left breast. Amba's doctor said that she'd need to have a one-inch square of tissue removed from her breast for a biopsy. Amba's inner authority or guidance was to work with the calcification holistically and avoid the invasive biopsy. Amba realized the doctor was afraid of being sued for malpractice and so she wrote a letter that she would not hold the doctor liable if there were any negative consequences from not getting a biopsy. The doctor relaxed and agreed. *We are not suggesting that this decision would be right for anyone else.* It was Amba's truth, guidance, and inner authority. One of the breakdowns of the medical model is that the doctor becomes the authority, the God, and the patient becomes the child. An updated model is that the doctor and patient, both coming from their inner authority, are collaborative partners working to enhance the health of the patient.

The foundation of living from inner authority is to follow the directive of the Oracle of Delphi: "Know Thyself." When we return to our own natures and know ourselves, we have the information we need to set ourselves free and to make a meaningful contribution to our world.

We have many inner voices. The voice of inner authority is often not the loudest or most familiar or even what the mind thinks. This voice may be quiet or it may be fierce. It is a sense of knowing, often with a feeling tone of integration, of settling in.

> Remember, all inner voices have a place at our table. Our capacity to embrace them all will allow us to move beyond them and hear the voice of our inner authority.

Quieting down often helps to hear the voice of inner authority. Use whatever way works for you to quiet down. It might be to walk, to sleep on it, to write, to listen to music, to pray, or meditate. When noise from your inner reactive voices has settled down, the voice of your inner authority can be heard, as an often quiet, mature, confident, and knowing voice.

When we are in our inner authority it is calming and integrative, as if our whole being is saying, "Yes." Later, when we think about the future and what following our inner authority might mean in our lives, the chorus of inner fears may strike up again.

Amba got very sick in 1998. She was too sick to go to her job as a full time physical therapist. It was time to decide if she was going to try to continue to work or quit. Her conflicting inner voices were very loud. Her inner fears said, "Who would I be without a job?" "Nobody." "I can't quit." "That would be lazy." "We need the money." "We will go into debt without this money." Conversely, the inner healer said, "I need to quit so that I can take care of myself, to let myself heal." And a practical voice: "I can't work. Every day I wake up and wonder if I'll be able to make it through the day."

Amba would go inside to access the voice of her inner authority. Time and again she would get the clear message: "It is time to quit and here is how you can go in and talk about it to your supervisors." Time and again, she would leave the quiet of her inner world and doubt the messages she had received. All hell would break loose inside her. All the conflicting voices would come screaming back. She would even walk out the door to go quit, and then turn around because she couldn't do it. Remember, all inner voices have a place at our table. Our capacity to embrace them all will allow us to move beyond them and hear the voice of our inner authority.

> **Following inner authority can be difficult. It often requires taking a stand.**

In Amba's process around quitting her job, she allowed each of her inner voices to scream their objections. The voice of the inner authority was consistent, clear, and strong. Eventually, given time, she trusted the clear calm voice of inner authority enough to take the step of action and quit the job. It was the right decision for her. Her health continued to deteriorate after quitting. It would take two years and all her available resources to recover enough to work again.

Amba made a decision long ago that she intended to follow

her inner authority. It connects her with her sense of Spirit, with her sense of the Divine, and with her path as a *love dog*. It is one of the most important components of her life. Following her inner wisdom represents her allegiance to her self. It brings her joy because it means living her life with an authentic connection to Spirit.

In many cultures ceremony is an important part of coming to inner authority. In modern society, it is up to us to create the ceremonies that help in our individuation. We have each individuated in our own lives in our own ways. You may recall your own such moments.

My husband, David, grew up in England and moved to Canada as an adult, partly to get away from a very controlling and very loving mother. Eight years later he wrote a letter to his mother saying that he was leading his own life, he was his own man, and he would no longer allow himself to be controlled by her directives. Even though he lived 5,000 miles away, his mother had not let go of him and David felt tethered to her until he created the ceremony of writing a letter of independence. It worked.

Years later when he returned to England to be with his dying mother, she said to him, "You were sick when you wrote that letter." He replied, "No, Mom, I was sick *until* I wrote that letter." This ceremony was David's initiation into manhood and the fruition of claiming his inner authority. Following inner authority can be difficult. It often requires taking a stand. I would encourage you to design ceremonies to help you formalize and celebrate the step of independence from following outer authority to following your own inner authority.

Even in nature there comes a time when animals must follow inner authority. When a bear is young and there is danger, the mother will swat the cub on the rear end and send it up a tree where it is safe. The cub learns through repetition that the way to deal with danger is to escape up a tree. This works well as long as the bear is young, but the bigger the bear grows, the less effective it is. As the bear gets heavier it becomes more difficult to find trees that will support its weight. At some point, the bear tries to climb a tree only to have it break under her weight. The bear must stop being allegiant to this teaching from its mother and find a new more appropriate way to handle adversity. The bear must stop climbing trees. It must run or turn and face its adversary. It must find the courage to live a new way.

I invite you to stand with the bear, to find and follow your own inner authority. As Shakespeare put it in *Hamlet*, "This above all: to thine own self be true."

Your sense of inner authority is the foundation for your capacity to relate to your partner as an equal. You and your partner can connect and live cooperatively to the extent that you have attained this emotional maturity. This means you are not blindly repeating patterns from the past but are writing a new story together, as the co-authors of your lives, using collaboration in relationship as a spiritual path.

In conclusion, I'd like to mention that your personal process of finding a way to become your own person, in and of yourself, sovereign in your own right, is an absolutely essential part of your maturation process. Without individuating and coming to terms with our inner authority, we act from old memories and live our lives from a position of psychological regression. When we discover who we are as adults and make choices based on that knowledge, we are so much more likely to live fulfilling lives and to be part of relationships where grown up meets grown-up (a *love dog* connection).

Let's remember that despite our childhoods, with all the wounding and sad stories, there is still, this very moment, a level of magnificence that lives in each of us. Leaving the familiar (that which we learned from our families) behind, learning how to integrate past wounding, and coming to discover who we are in our very essence are integral parts of embracing our humanity and vital parts of becoming *love dogs*. Claiming our inner authority is the foundation of sustaining a relationship with self, one another, and the Divine.

> In order to wake up, you have to first realize that you have been sleeping.
>
> —George I. Gurdjieff—

The Well of Grief

Those who will not slip beneath

the still surface on the well of grief

turning downward through its black water

to the place we cannot breathe

will never know the source

from which we drink,

the secret water, cold and clear,

nor find in the darkness glimmering

the small round coins

thrown by those who wished for

something else.

- David Whyte -

(Whyte, *Where Many Rivers Meet: Poems by David Whyte*.
Reprinted with permission.)

Walking Through Grief

My true purpose in writing this soul note is to invite other *love dogs* into the center of my current grieving process to demonstrate feeling grief with truth and passion. I want to share about my own grief because it clears my soul and lets the reader into my heartbreaking humanity, thus allowing us to meet here in these pages, *love dog* to *love dog*. When I grieve genuinely, I can go forward after loss and I'm able to love again. I want to demonstrate for you, dear reader, that in feeling our grief, we set ourselves free to go on living and loving.

> When I touch my grief and give it full expression it ALWAYS becomes a GIFT and it surely becomes part of the way I am connected, through the filter of my own compassion, to all those who are grieving.

I am open to deeply entering my grief because I have experienced countless epiphanies in the past when I move towards my feelings rather than away from them. As I experience and write about the emotions, they become my friends, rather than my adversaries. The feelings start to integrate; they become more a part of me; a homecoming celebration begins.

I made the promise to my husband and both my beloved animal companions that I would see them through to the end of their lives and promised to go on living and loving in their names. I believe that when our loved ones die that is what they really want: that we find a way to see them through and that we go on living and loving, for our own selves, and as a tribute to them.

Walk gently into this reading being both mindful and tender with yourself. This soul note may bring up some of your own feelings of unresolved grief. It may offer you a sense of how to be with yourself as you are grieving. This is my hope.

In this soul note I offer my recent journal account addressing my own grief cry. I then share a way to work with grief using reparenting. Hopefully, the poetry will open you to your own grief and then the journal writing and reparenting will offer you some tools to work through your own sadness.

Thank you for being open to another level of our heartbreaking/heartwarming humanity. If you can find a way to allow for grief, your capacity for all other emotions, including outrageous joy, expands. It's a bit like a water faucet—when we turn down the volume on feelings like fear, rage, hurt, shame, despair, and grief, we also, automatically turn down the faucet on all the rest of our feelings. Therefore, we shut off joy, passion, compassion, enthusiasm, excitement, and love. My choice is to open the faucet all the way and live the most authentic life possible for me to live. You get to make your own choice.

When I touch my grief and give it full expression it *always* becomes a *gift* and it surely becomes part of the way I am connected, through the filter of my own compassion, to all those who are grieving. *Love dog* to *love dog* we join hands in our common humanity and great grief cries!

Becoming a Love Dog

Journal Entry – February 27, 2007
Following is a letter to the God of my understanding, Tenderness, and to All the Ones Who Listen (my spiritual guides and soul friends.)

Dear Ones Who Listen:

I want to write about my dear husband, David, tonight. He was the answer to a prayer—truly. I asked You quite specifically, in the midst of a dark night of the soul, to either send visible proof of your presence, like a vision at the end of my bed that would talk to me aloud, or send a man who loved You and could be my life partner. I remember those moments as if it were yesterday. I was in that pining place and I really did not believe I could go on with my life's work as a psycho-spiritual counselor without this help, this very specific help.

That prayer was my deepest longing, my greatest truth. You answered. Within days David was stepping out of his rusty, old, green Comet automobile and running across my lawn in Seattle and I *knew* it was him. I could feel it in my very bones.

You picked the very best man in the entire world for me. David has been my lover, my friend, my mom and my dad, my sibling, my business partner, my advocate, my power match, my soul mate, and my husband.

I am deeply and profoundly grateful that you sent David to me and that he has been my greatest support for more than twenty years. And, I miss David as he was back when he was forty eight and I was thirty seven, more than twenty-four years ago.

I really rely on David. I count on him. His loyalty is my saving grace. And, he's getting old. He's ill now—cold, allergies, and an injured leg. He's really "spent," and while a part of me knows this is just a visit with his mortality and my pending loss—just a small visit—a larger part of me is in the early stages of a profound grief.

I am angry. He's not there for me. And I'm angry that he

needs me to be there for him.

I feel selfish.

I'm angry that I currently provide our financial resources and now I must be the nurturer as well.

I'm truly pissed off.

And, I'm sad. I miss his vitality and his humor and his strong arms. I miss his devotion to me. Right now all his attention is drawn inward.

A wiser one or perhaps just an older one within sees this aging process in him and honors him and is able to hold this space in his name.

Some younger and crankier ones in here are screaming to high heaven: "I can't do it. I won't do it. I don't want to be the grown up here."

"It's his job to take care of me."

"I don't want to turn the tables."

My brushes with aging and dying are relatively few. Daddy died suddenly when I was seven years old. My grandparents died within a month of one another when I was twenty. While I was part of their care team, I was also just leaving home and so I wasn't on the line through the end with them. Next my eldest sister, Jan, died and I was not living nearby so I was sheltered from her active dying process. Then my mom died and she was faltering for some time before I arrived on the scene. I was there for her last few days but I didn't really do the long haul. There were times I was impatient with her and I certainly do not look back on that experience as if I were a perfectly loving daughter.

On each of these other passings, I did play a part and I do see it was even a significant part. But, I was not the main one seeing the family member through. I was an "extra." In David's life I am his "person" and that frightens me. Since we don't have kids, or parents, or even relatives nearby, I'm scared. I'm already lonely and overwhelmed with this brief visit with illness.

Becoming a Love Dog

Here's the deal, *Dear Ones Who Listen*, I'm just praying that this is practice and I'm gaining experience because right now he only has a cold, allergies, and an injured leg. I feel so much emotion, all that I've already said and more, much more, cutting me deeper.

I never have seen a person all the way through. I did see my beloved white golden retriever, Grace, all the way through. All the way. Perhaps it's all practice just the same.

This is my first experience of being the primary support person for a life partner's aging and dying process. I am equally horrified and, someplace deeper down in the wellspring of my being, honored to walk this beloved man all the way through.

And, I do have a sense more of the time, way more of the time than I used to, that I am not alone. There are the unseen presences that come from ALL *You Who Listen:* Rumi, Hafiz, Papaji, Christ, and the One, that I have a sense are invisibly present for me.

And then there are all the countless other *love dog*s who stand by my side: Susan and Shell, Amba and Chittak, Carol, Stephi, Isabelle and Karin, Ashisha and Carolyn, the centering prayer and the twelve-step communities, and my sweet women's group, Sophia, Kate, and Gwen.

I am very willing to reach for whatever hands can hold mine as I hold his. It is my privilege to walk David through and I am absolutely not walking alone.

One last part of this early grief about David is that once he's gone, and since he's also "my" person, I'm worried about where the hands will come from that help see me through. I won't have a "person" though I will have a team. I will need to consider that Tenderness, the God of my understanding, can work through any hands that are willing.

The second phase of my grief right now is that Joli, my dear fifteen-year-old dog, who has spent ten of her years sharing life with us, is about to turn the corner to the other side. Of course, we too stand in the unknown—I don't know when she'll die. Sometimes she seems close and sometimes she seems far from the edge. When she's in the woods, her life force kicks in and she can still chase a rabbit even if it's only for a few moments.

> Maybe this is what "strong" looks like when tenderness is woven in: weeping even when death's relatives—illness and aging—show up. Maybe true strength is weeping before death is at the door. Maybe this really is all just a chance to practice dying.

She's suffering. I don't know how much. She can still hop on the bed most days and sometimes she needs a little help. She sleeps pretty well and she's still interested in her food, her treats, and her daily walks. She has the best medical and spiritual care any dog could have. We are doing all we know to see her through.

Joli is sweet, loyal, and kind and she has been my partner working with people for the past decade. She guards the door. Then she greets the clients. Then she holds the space for the soul work we do. She took over that job when Grace died. She is a dog and a *love dog*.

I'm sad. I'm deeply sad.

I needed to get away this weekend so that I could both escape my role as care giver and meet my grief. This monastic environment is cradling me so that I can meet my grief. When I'm at home being the primary caregiver for David and Joli, my grief lives in the background. Since I am in the middle of seeing them through, my perspective is shaped by the experience of being a caregiver and there is not much room for tending to the needs of my own soul.

I don't want Joli to die.

I hate death.

The unknown sucks.

I really want control.

In fact, "I demand, sweet Jesus, that you leave my man and my dog alone. Don't you dare, Death, knock on my door."

"Okay. So maybe you are not knocking yet, but you are in the neighborhood."

God, how I hate You.

God, how I wish I had the power to push You away.

And, God, dear God, oh, God—

In this place of early grieving I am equally grateful for every moment I spend, every single moment that I've spent with these two beloveds. I would not be willing to give up any of the moments I spent loving and being loved by Joli and David and by You, *Dear Ones Who Listen.*

Just to remind You, or perhaps to remind myself, I cannot, absolutely cannot, do these challenges without You at my side. I can't bear Joli's dying or even David's cold, allergies, sore leg, and loss of energy. I am so weak. (I am just not emotionally strong enough).

Or, maybe I am confused. I have, in my mind, a linear formula of how grief should look instead of allowing it it's own ever changing face. Maybe this is what "strong" looks like when tenderness is woven in: weeping even when death's relatives—illness and aging—show up. Maybe true strength is weeping before death is at the door. Maybe this really is all just a chance to practice dying.

I'll need more help than usual working with my clients, these souls you send. Perhaps you are on board every moment but I would really like to know that more. Send signs.

These tears I cry for David and Joli and for myself are holy tears. They are my measure of loving them. So, I am bowing towards Joli and David and allowing them both to crack this heart of mine even more wide open.

I return to Santa Fe in honor of my beloveds and I can't wait to join them now that I've had a chance to get this all off my chest.

> **The moment we truly love our grief, it becomes a kind of translucent joy.**

I must remember to take really good care of myself. I need my own spiritual strength, physical stamina, and emotional wherewithal to be with them. I need to gather my team closer and tend to myself more tenderly and consistently than ever before.

I guess it's really little Patti, my seven-year-old inner child, who thinks we can't do it and we have to do it alone. Let's talk to her before we close.

(For those of you who are new to these concepts, the following is an example where I, Patricia, reparent my little inner girl, Patti. Reparenting is the process where we become the parent to the little ones inside who didn't necessarily get the emotional and spiritual support they needed when they were young. Our adult, healthy, and wise self can now do this job.)

Dear Patti girl,
I love you, child of my heart.
I dearly and deeply love you.
Come sit on my lap and let me hold you.
I am so sorry for your many losses.
I'm here honey, lean into me.
That's right. Rest into my arms.

Sweetie, it's true that our puppy is getting older and she is on her way home and that means she'll be dying soon. She won't have a body any more. She will, though, remain close to us. You know how sometimes we feel Grace's sweet presence or we look in the mirror and see Grace's image reflected back in our eyes. Joli will be with us like that.

She'll be a sweet memory and a loyal friend on the inside.
Patti, I really welcome every tear. Every one. I love you.
I want to remind you, we are not alone. We have a great resource team and you can count on me to reach to every single one of them. Notice, dear girl, how I am already doing that now.
Way deep down inside, there are also the Ones Who Always Listen, our soul friends for years and years and years. They saw us through all the deaths to now. They sent other love dogs to nurture and care for us as we grieved. Remember that.
David is sick and I know you are scared and, honey, I don't think it's really his time yet. I believe he still has plenty of life force and he'll get well again. I can't promise this, but it's really my best guess. He's not terminal, he's ill.
I promise, Patti, that I'll see you through and that Tenderness will carry us.
Patti, you are always welcome here and remember, dear girl, you do have an inner mom and dad today who are very, very strong, with many resources, inside and out. You have one of the greatest support teams on earth.
Love, Patricia (your inner mom and dad)

In closing, I find that grief, at its onset, is experienced in primary colors—dominant, powerful colors that seem to take over the whole of our existence. For me, grief never really goes away. Sometimes, grief shifts towards the more pastel shades and then, in an instant, grief arises once again, bold and beautiful, and seemingly relentless.

Most of us have never really been taught how to grieve. Because our culture and our families usually teach us that the best thing to do after we have experienced loss is to turn away from our grief and get up and go on, we suffer more. Grief after grief piles up in our hearts until we are frozen and can't risk loving again. The only way to move from the emptiness of our grief cries into a place of tenderness for ourselves is by letting "it" all in and by letting "it" all out. Meltdowns, in my experience, are an excellent way to tap into our *love dog* nature.

It is my humble prayer that we would all consider turning towards our holy tears so that we can go on living and loving. For many of us an essential part of our soul's journey is to travel along with grief at our side, grief welling up in our eyes, and grief lumbering through our bodies. The moment we truly love our grief, it becomes a kind of translucent joy.

All honor to our grieving hearts.

Tenderly

Tenderly, I now touch all
things

knowing one day we will
part

—Saint John of the Cross—

(Ladinsky, *The Subject Tonight is Love - 60 Wild and Sweet Poems of Hafiz*. Reprinted with permission.)

ROUND WOMAN

My mom was a round woman
About 5' tall,
Maybe 200 pounds.

My mom's sisters, my aunties,
Were mostly round women,
Especially my Aunt Margaret.

I loved my Aunt Margaret best.
Sometimes when my mom was at work
Or traveling for politics
My Aunt Margaret would live with us
And care for us.

When I came home from school
There she would be
Eyes blazing
Arms open
Hugging me deeply and sweetly.

I would be folded into her bosom
And she would invite me to come to the table
For a snack and a game of canasta.

My Aunt Margaret had her stomach stapled three times
Because she lived in a culture that fed her the idea
That 'round is bad',
especially if you are a 'round woman,'
And 'fat is a sign of weakness.'

HAVING A POUCHY STOMACH is a bit like
BEING AN AX MURDERER!

I grieve for my Aunt Margaret
I walk over to her grave
And reach in and kiss those staples and unravel them
And fold myself back into that round woman's love.

I am a round woman.
**Is there anyone in the house who would walk
With me to put the staple gun down?**

—Patricia Flasch—

When Food Becomes a Substitute for Love

I wrote the poem, "Round Woman" in 2001. I hope it will open our hearts to the possibility of taking a stand against one of our deepest and most unaddressed cultural prejudices: the 'collective unconscious' judgment of body issues. Our culture regards fat people as despicable. This becomes a serious problem when we think we are fat. Becoming aware of our own grief about the way fat people are treated, we have a chance to reach a whole new level of body acceptance and self-love. Please join me on this transformational journey.

The topic of food and how we view our bodies is close to my heart, because I've spent so much time over the years locked in food obsession with no seeming hope of redemption. Though it's sad and scary to write about, I *know* many of us addictively use some kind of substance because we've lacked nourishment, attention, and the kind of parental support we really needed as children. Often we didn't get these things from our parents and our parents often missed the same things from their parents. We are talking about a multi-generational wound and potential healing.

My friend Sophia tells me that she has used food for years and years as her lover. While she also sees that there are many things she lacked growing up, she uses food in her life today to soothe the ache of a missing lover.

When Food Becomes a Substitute for Love

We are focusing on food addictions in this soul note, but the ideas here apply to all the addictions. Addressing our compulsions gives us the chance to stop feeling separate from ourselves, one another, and the "God of our own understanding." Once we feel closer to ourselves, our *love dog* nature becomes a more constant part of our experience of being alive and we step into greater and greater feelings of tenderness for ourselves.

Most clients in my private practice have, on some level, a food, drug, alcohol, sex, relationship, or work addiction. I believe these addictions arise out of our feeling of not enough-ness. This is a part of what I call "the big black inner hole" that we try with all of our might to avoid. This big black hole we try to fill also contains the belief, "I don't have enough to survive!"

Pause for a moment, and ask yourself the question. What is your relationship with food (or sex, work, drugs, alcohol, etc.) really about? Is it your parent, protector, safety, lover, or best friend? What is it for you?

Because my deepest experience is that food has become my parents, I will spend most of my time writing about that aspect of food addiction. Please take these concepts and apply them to your particular history and circumstances.

My mom was the youngest of eight children during the depression and her father was blind. It was hard. How could she possibly have gotten what she needed physically or emotionally or spiritually? She truly didn't have enough; she felt the pain of not having enough and unconsciously passed on to her children the idea that "there is not enough." This is a multigenerational message and one that represents more than 50% of the people in our world who really don't have enough. It's impossible to care about your self-esteem if you don't know whether or not you are having something to eat today.[*]

---

[*] According to Abraham Maslow's hierarchy of needs, when we don't have our survival needs met (food, shelter, water, health care etc.) we can't possibly concern ourselves with emotional or spiritual needs.

Becoming a Love Dog

My mother and I, and all the rest of us, have pain that we are trying to cover up or avoid in some substantial way. That inner black hole, covered over by an addictive process, is central to our human condition. Remember, dear reader, do not think, "I'm bad for having pain or for attempting to cover it over with food or another substance." Think instead, "I am human and I am not always able to look in the face of my own pain. I'm on a journey of discovering how to be with my core emotions one day at a time."

I believe that the inner black hole we are so desperate to fill is about more than the pain of childhood and what we are taught. *I believe that our primal pain is our separation from the Divine. I think that 'missing' our parents, partners, friends, and animals, reinforces that deep feeling of spiritual disconnection.*

In our attempt to avoid that black hole of pain, we stuff ourselves with a substance that we hope will numb our pain. For me, *every time* I overeat I experience a momentary high, followed by gobs of shame.

That feeling of emptiness or void that I want to cover over remains buried within me. Now it's covered over with shame as well. *My **mind** knows absolutely that this food will not, absolutely will not, cover up the pain more than a nanosecond. Yet I slip many times into the fantasy that it will.*

The poet Robert Bly, in his book, *A Little Book on the Human Shadow*, has a chapter on "the long bag we drag behind us." The idea is that we are all given an invisible bag when we are born. We place in that bag the emotions we don't want to feel and the parts of ourselves we find unlovable. As we age we keep throwing more and more unacceptable parts into the bag and it gets bigger and heavier. It may get so heavy we can't carry it anymore. At some point in our lives, we might be forced to stop and look in the bag.

Many of us are so desperate not to look into that long bag that we distract, numb, and soothe ourselves with food, sex, drugs, work, and so on. But the truth is, when we spend our lives refusing to look into that bag, it's a bit like being invited to a feast and refusing to sample some of the dishes. Being willing to taste all the dishes, experience all that we are, allows us to be the full, rich, diverse, unique *love dogs* we really are.

> **We can work with this, we can work it through. We do not, do not, have to accept a life lived from shame and self-condemnation.**

I am aware of the painful story that parts of me are unacceptable, that I don't have enough to survive, that I am separate. All of these old stories that I've been listening to for so many years are just that—stories. I think I'm separate from my body. I think I'm separate from God. I've dreamed that what I eat or what I look like matters in the mind of *The Ones I Hold Most Dear*. I've slipped into a place of human separation. It's not my spiritual truth and it's not *the* spiritual truth, but they are familiar lies that live lurking in the background of my memory and subconscious mind.

I *know* that the spiritual truth is that my body is a vessel, carrying me through life, in Service to my eternal Spirit. My living spiritual practice is to become partners with my body.

Here is a poem I wrote several years ago called "Chocolate Chip Cookies." It expresses the kinds of things that I believe lurk in my subconscious mind and possibly in your mind as well. Once I bring them up and out and share them with you, they no longer have the same hold on me that they do when they are rattling around inside my mind. If you've suffered with compulsive overeating, you will relate to this poem:

CHOCOLATE CHIP COOKIES

Rich brown chocolate
slipping and sliding down my throat
brown sugary, white flowery dough
lathered round the chips
vanilla smell transporting me
to sweet times past in
Grandma's kitchen
nuts and creamy butter mixing
to form these decadent morsels
of morning delight.

Danger lurks ominously
in the background of my mind
before we finish the first round.
Ten cookies have more power
than Saddam Hussein and
all his oil
to catapult me into mountains
of green gooey shame
and dark disdain.

Years of torment
wash over me
for breaking the rules
not counting the calories
adding flab to my hips
or my gut
and flipping the bird
at years of restraint
dressed up in propriety
left licking the grate.

Creeping slowly to bed
dreaming dreams of reprisal
that would put Hitler to shame.

When Food Becomes a Substitute for Love

What I appreciate about this poem is that it expresses my experience of being in the midst of the old body shame story. I love that the poem offers no answers. I love that the poem is a simple expression of my heartbreaking humanity. I know there are many other *love dogs* out there, now reading this soul note, who know this kind of shame. Part of my purpose in writing this chapter is to remind you, dear ones, that you are not alone. My further purpose is to let you know *we can work with this, we can work it through. We do not,* **do not***, have to accept a life lived from shame and self-condemnation.*

One of my dearest friends in the world, Stephani, is a woman who could easily be on the cover of Cosmopolitan or Yoga Journal. She is truly beautiful. Here is Stephani's story in her own words.

I strung wire through the spaces between my four back teeth on either side of my jaw. I learned to talk with my teeth clenched waiting tables helping to support my husband through graduate school. I unwired my jaws weekly to clean my mouth and binge on pastries by taking bites over the sink, chewing them, and spitting them out.

I wish I could say I had healed my eating disorder, but I cannot. One difference is that these days when I have to get out my "fat" pants, two sizes larger than my "regular" pants, which I have had to do recently, I don't beat myself up about it or get hysterical inside. I see it as a barometer for my stress level and it makes me sad.

I believe Stephani's compulsive eating is rooted in a childhood that included frequent and heated arguments between her parents. As the arguments became more intense, her parents moved towards separation and divorce, Stephani, like me, and so many other *love dogs*, turned to food to fill the void she was experiencing in her home life. It's easy to understand today that food cannot replace parents, or parental love, and it cannot really soothe us to make up for the heartache in our home lives. While our minds may understand, our bodies have a pattern of using food to stuff feelings and to serve as a substitute for love. Stephani still has the habit of using food at times, and she has created some room inside herself for forgiveness and her own redemption.

> **Self-condemnation does not heal addictions.** Addictions are healed in the context of greater self-compassion and growing self-esteem, which allow us to take actions that are more caring and suitable for our own wellbeing.

I'm so very sorry, dear Stephani, that you starved yourself in an attempt to please your husband, yourself, and this weight-obsessed culture. I'm so sorry and I love you. And, I'm also sorry for the part of me that is exactly like you and that goes that far—the one in each of us that will wire our jaws shut and drink liquids to try to silence the voices of shame and stop the self-hatred that we are habitually stuck with. My heart goes out to all of us who share this problem. I am so very sorry and I love you. Thank you, Universe, for bringing this to all of our attentions for transformation and healing.

I have another very dear friend who is seventy-five and living in Colorado. Her dilemma is that she either ends up hating herself for eating "too much" and weighing "too much" *or* she ends up feeling desperate because she is drinking only the liquid diet prescribed by her doctor. So she's either shaming herself or depriving herself. Of course, she thinks this is all her fault. She doesn't really see that our culture gives us conflicting messages: EAT MORE *and* STAY THIN. When we try to do both, most of us end up feeling trapped emotionally. Accepting these cultural messages is more the cause of emotional pain for my sweet seventy-five-year-old friend than childhood neglect. I feel mounds of sadness, followed by endless compassion for this dear *love dog*.

My friends, like most of us, have several levels of problems.

When Food Becomes a Substitute for Love

The first level is using food or whatever else it is we use to avoid feelings. The second and much larger problem is the internal voices that club us for having the problem. These voices lead to a feeling of spiritual disconnection. *Self-condemnation does not heal addictions.* Addictions are healed in the context of greater self-compassion and growing self-esteem, which allow us to take actions that are more caring and suitable for our own wellbeing.

Lacking love or support is not an adult excuse to go on bingeing. Bingeing is a boundary-less place and it doesn't serve our bodies or our beings. Yet, if we have slipped, it is more helpful to move towards self-soothing rather than self-criticism. The quicker we can be kind to ourselves, the quicker we can step towards healthy boundaries in our eating.

I want to share parts of my personal history, so I can offer you a connection with my journey to food becoming a substitute for love. I am aware I reap many benefits as I share my own story. (It would foster a deeper self-understanding and self-compassion for you to write your own history specifically related to the use of food, or other addictions, to fill emotional holes.)

In my life, the death of my dad when I was seven and the subsequent emotional death of my mom really did lead to making food a substitute for parental love. Most of us have had real losses that have contributed to our addictive patterns.

I remember when I was ages seven to twelve, though I was skinny as a rail, I used to eat four pieces of toast and four fried eggs for breakfast. Early in the month, when the paycheck still stretched, I might follow that up with a few glazed donuts. I often made my own meals and the meals for my little sister while my mom was working.

We were, at times, "latch key" kids, and food was a vital part of our coping mechanisms. Neither my little sister nor I got fat then because we lived next door to a playground and spent our days running, playing baseball, and swimming. It was a lonely existence without parents. Thank God for our grandparents and Aunt Margaret who became our companions when Mom had to work.

Both Grandma and Aunt Margaret nurtured us with schaum tortes and lemon meringue pies and piles of popcorn and candy. I mean no disrespect to my grandparents, parents, or my dear aunt; it's just that food, back then, and sometimes the lack of it, was an elemental part of what we built our family culture around. I went to my grandparent's house because I felt deeply loved by them and they lit up when I arrived. I also came to associate love (from Grandma and Grandpa) with sweets and treats. I don't really like admitting this, but there are many parts of me that still agree that *sweets are equal to love*. It is, after all, a cellular memory.

When I turned twelve and hit puberty, I began developing and gaining weight, which was very frightening for me. We are taught that what we look like is more important than who we are. The hard part is that I lived, and still live, in a culture that both pushes eating lots of junk food and advertises over and over again that being thin is our ultimate goal. We are living in a constant state of confusion over this mixed message. How can we both EAT MORE *and* STAY THIN?

Though I was terrified of gaining weight, partly because I lacked long-term nourishment from my parents, I continued to look to food as my Source. A simple way of saying this would be to say that *food became a substitute for love, and food became God.* That pattern still lives and breathes in my experience when I feel that I compulsively need to eat.

I can easily use food in an unconscious way, seeking soothing, just as a child wants to be loved. I use it to deal with sadness, or grief, or fear, or guilt, or worry, or anxiety, just about any emotion really. I can use food to suppress joy, love, passion, or creativity. Food helps me in my attempt not to feel powerful emotions all across the spectrum.

When Food Becomes a Substitute for Love

Many times I don't really know why I had to have those extra carbohydrates before bed. I look back in the morning and discover the truth: I wasn't hungry for food; I was hungry for soothing.

> **Naming what I need and then giving it to myself *always* calms me down and moves me out of the arms of food obsession and into a place of spiritual, emotional, and physical balance with myself.**

While my skills in the self-soothing department have grown immeasurably through the years, my habit of eating comfort food stills arises right along side and often trumps the one who knows how to comfort myself without using food.

I do know on an intellectual level, and I do know much of the time on an emotional level, that food will not fill the void. I do *know* that a vital part of my spiritual path as a *love dog* is to be willing to meet all of those feelings that are part of my heartbreaking humanity. My growing ability to make room for my own emotions allows me to have a much wider range for your emotions.

I need to pause briefly and acknowledge my feelings of despair and disgust that I am not further along my journey and *only* eating in moderation and balance. The critical parent shouts, "What's wrong with you, you are sixty years old. When will you get a handle on this? You are a poor excuse for a personal growth teacher. You fail to meet my standards over and over again. I despise you."

The little one cringes in response to this old refrain from my critical parent. Little Patti just retreats, her tears are on the inside and she is full of hopelessness. After all, she has been *verbally abused* about this food thing for decades. What is true today though is that my adult skill set is quickly available when I hear the shouting of the internal critic and the cries of my wounded girl. I notice within moments that the cellular memories kick in that say I'm bad for eating whatever it is I think I should not be eating, and then my little one cries reactively. I notice quickly, and moments later my wise woman steps in and says:

Wow, wait a minute! You've gone off on that trip about food and shame. Stop it! It doesn't work and it hurts! Instead let's pause and remember that we love our body and ourselves despite our struggles with food. A kinder, clearer approach would be more helpful. What if we take a look to see what's up inside and then maybe we could see what it is that we need right now.

Most of the time I do get an answer to that question of what it is I need. And *the answer is almost always some form of emotional, physical, or spiritual replenishment.* The answer this time is "I need to hear an inner conversation that is kind, clear, and flexible. On the physical plane I need a nap. I need a large glass of water with a twist of lemon. I need a large green salad with many colorful veggies and a few nuts and some garbanzo beans." Naming what I need and then giving it to myself *always* calms me down and moves me out of the arms of food obsession and into a place of spiritual, emotional, and physical balance with myself.

Here is a poem I wrote about those unconscious, unmet needs.

When Food Becomes a Substitute for Love

The Influence of Unmet Needs

Get out of here, unmet needs.
Don't you dare show your face.
You have no right
to show up in my dreams,
come out sideways
or make me spend hours thinking my "answer"
is in the refrigerator
or in a glass of wine
or in a man.

I have tried to annihilate you, unmet needs.
I have suppressed you under the floorboards.
I have eaten you alive
and I have ignored you throughout time.

Yet, you have stayed on,
persistent, patient, and true,
living in my core,
dancing at my door.
You have spoken softly
like a rose petal
gently falling from the bloom.

And you have hollered on,
past my inner war.
And you have stood strong and tall
like the redwoods,
trusting the Universe
to begin answering your call.

Becoming a Love Dog

I wonder if all the plus-size women and extra large men have unconsciously made food "a substitute for love" in an attempt to soothe those hidden, unmet needs. I wonder how much of the super sizing and bingeing some of us have been doing actually has to do with something much deeper? Are we looking first for a love we didn't get while growing up? Is it even deeper? Are we looking for our own love? God's love? What's at the bottom of the extra large sack of french fries? My experience is EMPTINESS. They didn't fill me up. If I went around and around the take-out order window throughout the night, I believe that at the bottom of every bag of fries would be the great void.

I remember a time in high school when I went with four or five other friends to a local drive-in one night after school. We decided we would have a "who could eat the most hamburgers contest." I won the contest topping off at fourteen hamburgers. Perhaps this was just a teenage prank. On the other hand, I knew, even then, it was an attempt to fill the void of missing my dad and knowing he wouldn't be home when I got there nor would my mom because she was working. Of course, the silly prank did not take care of the void; it just gave me one mother of a stomachache followed by shame.

When I say we may have "unconsciously" made food "a substitute for love," I mean that we don't know what we are doing. This is not encouragement to blame our self; rather, it is an encouragement to find our deeper reasons for compulsive eating. When we don't know what is fueling this compulsion to eat, the chances of getting the compulsion to lessen are minimal.

Let me talk about compulsion as it relates to the topic of addictive eating. Compulsion is an irresistible impulse to act, regardless of the rationality of the motivation. Compulsive eating is an act we perform in response to this impulse to act.

While we may 'think' we can stop eating at any moment, the impulse to continue is larger than the mind's ability to make a new decision. It's a bit like when we are making love—we always have an opportunity to say, "No." "I don't want to go further into this." "Stop." "I need to talk for awhile." We have that choice at any point in the lovemaking process *except* once the orgasm has begun and the impulse to climax is in full force, it's no longer possible to say, "Stop" or, "I changed my mind." The innate impulse to orgasm is stronger than any decisions we might make.

> **You are not alone in struggling with this issue. Most human beings use something as a coping mechanism. Have compassion for us all. It's not that we're bad. It's that we are human and we often do not know how to meet our emotional or spiritual needs.**

That's my experience with compulsive eating. There is a point at which I can't seem to stop. I'll have to finish the bag of chips or the pint of ice cream, because I am no longer in charge and the compulsion has taken over and I'm a goner. I do notice that throughout the years I have learned to buy the smallest bag of chips and get the children's size cone at the ice cream parlor. *While the compulsion, and the inner void, is not always gone, it has lessened its grip on me.* I know that's because of the emotional and spiritual work I do to fill myself up, to feel my feelings and to stay connected inside to *The Ones I Hold Most Dear*.

Since it's unlikely that we are going to be able to fulfill the longing to retrieve what we lost in our long ago pasts, we can discover other ways to meet those old, unmet needs for love and nurturing. I am not saying that "food becoming a substitute for love" is the *only* reason we compulsively overeat, it's just a primary reason. You might pause a moment and check in with yourself. Was it and is it true for you that you have been eating to try to fill the emotional needs that were unmet in your younger days? If that's not it for you, what is it? What drives your compulsive eating or drinking or spending or shopping or shoplifting? What is it really? You'll find that answer somewhere within your own inner experience.

I have noticed that what starts out as early unmet needs, and results in a myriad of emotional issues including using food, is really stemming from a spiritual issue. Beneath the longing for our parents, for our families to remain in tact, for our brother or sister not to die of cancer, is also a spiritual void.

This may be a controversial issue for you. If so, please know that I deeply respect and honor your opinions whether we agree or not. My opinion is that what I've always been searching for in that void, deeper even than the longing for my parents, is God. I have forgotten that I cannot disconnect with God no matter whether I can *feel* God's presence in this moment or not. I have a deep, intuitive yearning to experience my union with the Divine. Though it's right in front of me and all around me and I am surrounded by the love of God; I still dream I'm disconnected.

I think again of the Rumi poem about *love dogs*. I am so comforted by Rumi's reminder that my loneliness and longing actually connect me to my Source. "Listen to the moan of a dog for its master. That whining *is* the connection."

If you consider yourself a *love dog*, you have this deep yearning as well. At the bottom of all my desires, even my burning lust for food, is my longing to feel connected.

Many, many years ago, I realized that I alone could absolutely not fix compulsive eating. I could not return to the womb of my mother's love or the arms of my father's devotion through food. It's only my connection with God that can do that. I don't mean a God up in the sky or an external God; I mean the deeply abiding presence of the God that lives within. (Note: this is the God of my understanding, not necessarily the readers.)

One of the ways I can sooth the pain of separation and unmet needs is to tune in to my inner wise woman, who is always connected with the Divine. My wise one, the most balanced part of me, has a much different perspective on the concept of "food becoming a substitute for love." She says the following:

Hey Patricia:

I'm so glad that you've decided to write about this topic because it has caused you more heartache than almost any other part of your life. I want you to remember you are part of a culture where one of the few remaining socially acceptable prejudices is against "fat" people. You are being influenced 100,000 times a day to eat more and stay thin.

Your addict screams, "MORE, MORE, MORE," though we know "MORE" will never be enough.

You are not alone in struggling with this issue. Most human beings use something as a coping mechanism. Have compassion for us all. It's not that you're bad. It's that you are human and you often do not know how to meet emotional or spiritual needs.

I want to appreciate how far you've come with this part of your humanity. Think of all the times you were truly kind today when you spoke to yourself about food or your body. Think of all the times you have learned to self-soothe. Think of all the support you have when you can't remember to be kind. Instead of noticing the times you've been off the mark (slipping away from moderation with food) think of all the times you have been moderate with food. In fact, most days you are moderate with food. You generally eat three balanced and moderate meals a day.

While it's true you seem to slip into a carb haze in the early evening, and you do want to address that and see what's going on, that does not make you a mortal sinner.

The God of Our Understanding, which is Tenderness, does not ever say, "You ate twenty-five sugarless chocolate-coated almonds last night. Now get off my lap." Tenderness says: "I love you, sweet woman, when you are in moderation and when you are not. You always have a place on my lap. My love for you is eternal and your love for yourself is growing and growing. Bless the one inside who craves attention or love and then thinks food will provide it. It's just a part of you that has forgotten that your true nurturing comes from Me in connection with you, my dear love dog *woman."*

As you continue to find places in your heart for a wider range of feelings, you will continue to move towards moderation with food.

Do you remember way back in the late seventies when you lived in the spiritual growth community and you were practicing that method called "conscious reprogramming?" Wow, that was intense. You'd yell and yell with a wastebasket over your head, "I love my body the way it is!!!!!!!!! I love my body the way it is!!!!!!!!! The echo for that affirmation would reverberate in your head. But you KNEW, didn't you, that you could shout that affirmation through eternity and that would not make it TRUE. The truth was that you hated your body the way it was.

Back then, you didn't have the skill to realize that the body thoughts were JUST thoughts, that the self-shame was a habit, nor that there were layers of self-forgiveness that would need to be done. You surely did not understand how often food had become a substitute for love. You were young, and yet deeply committed to your healing path even back then.

Today, let's remember that the majority of the time you really do love this beautiful, sweet, round, aging body. The percentage of time you spend thinking you have to change continues to diminish.

And there is a wellspring of forgiveness that lives in the center of your Self that is never very far away from "Ho'oponopono, Patricia. I am so very sorry that you've slipped into that old habit of judging your body. I am sorry, dear one, and I love you. I love you right in the midst of this old shame attack. Please forgive my harsh judgments of you. Thank you for calling this to my attention for healing. We offer all the old memories to the Universe for healing and transformation."**

With love from your Inner Wise Woman.**

** Talking to myself in this way is an example of the reparenting process.

Becoming Partners with Our Bodies

One of the main concepts I'd like to communicate in this soul note is that we can partner with our bodies and become allies rather than enemies. A wonderful way to start a partnership with our bodies is to write them a love letter telling them we would like to be partners. Here is the partnership love letter I wrote to my body.

Dear Body of Patricia:

I am inviting you with my whole heart into a new partnership. I am asking if, even after my own and the media's near constant abuse, you could find it within you to forgive me. I am so deeply sorry for hurting you and judging you and slamming you from so many directions. Please accept my apology.

Please know, sweet body, that I love you. I am making a decision to love you in a larger and clearer way than ever before. I promise to begin each day checking in with you to see how you are doing and what you need. I promise to provide you what you need, or as close an approximation as I can come up with. I am very sincere about loving you.

> We can partner with our bodies and become allies rather than enemies.

Let me say a few things to remind you about my choice to love you. You are beautiful. You are glorious. You have been so very good to me. I see that you are strong and vibrant. I notice that you are round and curvy and that you walk in a kind of melody. I love and accept you exactly as you are.

From the top of your head to the tips of your toes, I apologize for every single judgment I've sent your way. I'm so deeply sorry for the times I've judged your hair, your brains, your nose, your teeth, your eyes, your arms and legs and hips, your tummy and breasts, your butt, your feet, your internal organs, your poor knees, even your cells. I am so sorry for this habitual pattern of picking on you and so deeply hurting you.

Please accept my apology. Please know I am sincere.

Beloved body, sweet self, I am sorry and I do love you and please forgive me. Thank you for calling this to my attention for healing. I now give over all of the old memories and unconscious material related to my body to the Divine for transformation and healing.

In tenderness, Patricia

Please consider writing your own open letter to your body. Even if you cannot honestly say, "I love you, dear body," you can say, "I am learning to love you, sweet body." That will always be true because you are learning just by virtue of reading this soul note.

Let's take this idea of partnering with our bodies deeper. One way to begin is to start feeling our feelings rather than trying to stuff them with food. When I make the choice to be with the emotional pain and I allow myself to feel grief or anger or emptiness or despair, and just sit with it, I am so much more calmed, so much more present than when I try to ignore it or soothe it with food. I begin to realize that every emotion has a birth, a life, and a death. The younger part of me thinks that I will be swallowed up by whatever powerful emotion I am experiencing, but the adult part sees that feelings have a cycle just like seasons. The child believes when I am happy that I will always be happy and when I am sad, I will remain in sadness endlessly. My inner adult, though, knows that change is the way of the world, and "this too shall pass."

> **My greatest resource is my own inner, wise woman self. She is my ally and I need to remain conscious of her availability and presence in my life.**

It is my experience that our lives work better when we allow ourselves to experience our emotions. Then why can't we consistently be with our emotions? Why do we run from our human condition as if it's a house on fire? The *fear* of feeling the amount of grief or fear we actually carry is so uncomfortable we believe we can't tolerate it. On the other hand, every time, every single time, I have allowed myself to sit with a feeling and stay with it and let it rise and fall, I am more at peace. When I allow for the feeling, the allowance itself is a form of self-forgiveness. Even in the moments that I have been bent over with grief, my tears work their way through me when I allow them to flow freely. I call these "holy" tears.

Something else that has been very helpful in learning to partner with my body is to ask myself the question, "What am I hungry for?" Whew, I have been astounded at how often when I ask this question, the answer is not in the refrigerator. Here are a few examples of asking myself that vital question in the last few days. "What are you hungry for? A walk in the woods. What are you hungry for? A poem or two. What are you hungry for? Coconut juice. What, sweet woman, are you hungry for? Someone to listen to me for ten minutes as deeply as I have been listening all day long. What, beloved body, are you hungry for? A foot rub. What are you hungry for? Playing ball with my puppy. What are you hungry for? Closing my eyes and putting a soothing eye bag over them for as long as I want."

This might be the time to consider asking yourself, "What am I hungry for?" The next part is, of course, to give yourself what it is you are longing for or as close an approximation as you can. I might not be able to drop everything and head for a walk in the woods, but I can definitely walk around the block and I can plan a hike in the woods for next weekend.

Let's go back to the beginning of this soul note. Do you remember when I ended the round woman poem by saying, "Is there anyone in the house who would walk with me to put the staple gun down?"

The woman who wrote that poem is my Higher Self. She is a resource within me every time my old memories kick in about food and my body. She *knows* how to work with those voices. My greatest resource is my own inner, wise woman self. She is my ally and I need to remain conscious of her availability and presence in my life.

Finding a strong, supportive inner ally is another way we can move toward being partners with our bodies. To do this, first of all, think of who might be such an ally. Do you have a part of yourself that believes in you irrespective of your size? If you do, listen to her. If you cannot find that part of yourself, imagine a mentor who believes in you beyond your body image. This mentor might be someone who is alive and active in your life or it may just be a being that you create with your imagination, give this being all the qualities you need her to have so that she can be your ally in neutralizing your war with food and your body. Your ally can be your own highest Self, or it might even be a totem of some kind, like a sacred rock or any object that you consider holy. You can use this ally to draw strength and energy from as you heal from your food and body issues.

Next, consider all of the different voices you might have going on in your subconscious mind and in your memory body that relate to food and your body. This might include what you learned from your parents, teachers, friends, the media, glamour magazines, spouses, and so on. Pick one voice or thought that is particularly painful that you would like some input on.

Now, simply ask your inner ally for her point of view. You will be amazed at the wisdom you have inside just waiting to express itself. There are some simple steps you can take to help access the voice of your inner ally if you find this difficult. You might, for example, assign a location to each voice. The painful voice that says you are unacceptably fat might be assigned to the kitchen chair and the voice of the ally stands in front of the window. Now, physically move between the two positions and allow the voices to have a dialogue, out loud. It can be very helpful to do this with a supportive friend. You can help each other focus and it will ensure you actually set aside the time to do the process. If you are writing in a journal, try assigning each voice it's own color pen.

Here are some examples of how the process works in my own life, starting with an old, painful belief: My mom truly utterly believed that if she were not thin and beautiful she would lose my father. If she lost my father, she would not survive since he was the provider. For her, trying to stay thin and beautiful was a *survival issue*. I took on my mom's survival issue and the message that I would die if I did not remain thin and beautiful. When I ask my inner ally, the one who wrote the round woman poem, what she thinks, she has a whole other viewpoint. My wisest self says, "We do not have to be any particular way to be lovable," and "We have many, many things to offer this world irrespective of our physical appearance." She also says, "Our body, right now, is beautiful!"

The next voice that emerges for me is the voice of my addiction. She screams, "MORE, MORE, MORE! I WANT MORE. I want to eat a plate full, a room full, a city full of Cheetos and potato chips and pizza. It will never be enough."

> **Your body is your *perfect weight* the moment you decide, *"I'm good as I am. I love myself this moment."***

Again, if I return to my ally, she sings a different song. She sings that there is no answer to the MORE challenge. She advises that I just allow myself to feel my craving, pining song and then go ahead and love my broken-hearted addicted self as deeply as I can. "I love you, one who screams, 'MORE, MORE, MORE.' And I know that the only way to fill the cup is inside. Cheetos won't do it, but true tenderness for you will do it!"

The voice of addiction, the voice that says, "EAT MORE" is utterly seduced by the cultural messages from McDonalds, Burger King, Pizza Hut, Kentucky Fried Chicken, Baskin Robbins, and on and on and on. My ally from the round woman poem says, "We don't have to be influenced by the mass media's message that we won't survive if we don't stuff ourselves with whatever food product they are selling. We can mute the commercial and we can walk away from the hype."

Someday I'll write a poem titled, "I wanted Kentucky Fried, So Bad, I Nearly Died." So far I just have the title, but it will show how our survival issues are linked up with the media's incessant messages.

The media messages from the other direction are just as strong. In our country there is a multi-billion dollar diet industry. This industry has taught us well. What they would like us to believe is that if we don't do Jenny Craig or Weight Watchers or the weight "solution" de jour, we will not survive. Is that the spiritual truth? It's time for each *love dog* to ask that question. Have we come here for this time on earth to *look good* or have we come here to find our way *home*? If the latter is true, then our own mercy is what we most need. If looking good is still what is most important for you, then be honest about that, pick up another diet plan, and love yourself and have mercy for yourself.

The final inner voice I will share is the voice of the war itself. "I MUST HAVE MORE versus I CAN'T HAVE MORE BECAUSE I MUST BE THIN." It's my job, with the help of my inner wise woman, to befriend them both. I need to *bless and forgive* the "I MUST HAVE MORE" voice and *bless and forgive* the "I MUST BE THIN" voice. It's my personal work to find my way to *moderation*. What is just enough food? Can I take the gigantic risk of loving my body right now without changing a thing? Can you? Let's learn how to befriend our bodies together.

Please, let your ally stand up and be counted. Your ally can remind you that there really is no "perfect weight" nor is there an answer outside you to the deeper longing behind the craving that lives inside you. Your body is your **"perfect weight"** the moment you decide, "*I'm good as I am. I love myself this moment.*"

I encourage you to take the steps to first discover and then really listen to your inner ally. Then, let all the voices of your humanity show up so that you can hear them.

Once you can hear them, they can be forgiven and released.

Here is a lovely line from a Hafiz poem called "The Woman I Love" that might comfort us as we work to make peace with our bodies.

> **The Beautiful One whom I adore
> has pitched His royal tent
> inside of you.**

Love dog to *love dog*, and irrespective of our human condition and our issues with food or any other substance, I do believe that we are looking to find that feeling, the spiritual knowingness, that God has pitched Her royal tent inside of us, this moment, just as we are.

I want to offer as many strategies as I can for shifting from "food has become a substitute for love" to "we've remembered our connection with the Divine and we can sustain that connection most of the time." My favorite step from the twelve-step programs, and the one I shall carry with me, close to my heart, throughout my lifetime is the eleventh step. It says, "We sought through prayer and meditation to improve our conscious contact with God, as we understand God, praying only for the knowledge of His/ Her will for us and the power to carry that out."

Beginning my days with prayers and meditation and offering all my heartbreaking humanity into the arms of the *Ones I Hold Most Dear* means that I'm operating with an open heart and it's no longer "me" steering the ship. Instead the part of me that is deeply connected with the Divine is guiding me across the ocean.

Putting my hand in God's hand and asking for help each day, not only with my food but also with all the things that trouble me, means that I feel the presence of grace throughout my day. When I ask that I be able to be a hollow flute for all those I touch that day, I place myself in Service. Once I am in that place of Service, the day becomes much more open hearted and my unmet needs recede into the background. The day shifts towards the clients and students I work with, sorting out their unmet needs and supporting them to find their own place of inner wholeness.

Another way of shifting away from "food being a substitute for love" is to make eating a part of our spiritual path. When I can remember to dedicate my meals to *The Ones I Hold Most Dear*, I'm much more likely to chew and taste the food and to feel nourished at the end of the meal rather than stuffed.

Last night I ate at one of the local organic cafes. I was in a centered place and I was able to say grace in my own way before I ate. I then had a wonderful experience tasting and slowly chewing the greens, yam, and burnished tofu covered in ginger sauce. It was exquisite food, and since I was paying attention, I only ate half the food and brought the rest home for breakfast. I am learning to cherish my growing experiences with moderation and to forgive myself more quickly when I eat in excess.

As I conclude this soul note I am filled with connection and mercy for you, dear reader and myself. My deepest wish for us all is that we fall into the fire of our own undaunted mercy. May we laugh and cry together about the games our minds play as they pretend that we are separate from *The Ones We Hold Most Dear*, separate from ourselves, and separate from one another.

TO THE LUMPS THAT LIVE ON MY HIPS

I am certainly surprised
that you still hang out
on the top of my legs and the
side of my body.
Can't you take a hint?

I have cursed you,
ignored you,
shamed you in mirrors
(for decades,)
stuffed you in girdles,
and blamed you for low
self-esteem and sexual
inadequacies.
I mean, really, what does it take
for you to get it?
GET LOST YOU DISGUSTING SACK OF FLAB!!!!!!!!!!!!

Can you find it in yourself
to forgive my utter ignorance?
This will probably come as a shock
to you, so late in life,
BUT I would genuinely like to start over
and see if we could be friends.
I just didn't know any better.
I didn't understand that

Becoming a Love Dog

you have been my buffer,
my protection from attention
I did not want to receive,
and, a most familiar place
to rest my troubles.

Now, I would like to honor your persistence
in waiting at the table UNTIL I could join
you and we could share this feast of life
and light a candle of compassion
for all those women still lost
in this endless strife, in this hip-hating life.

*PS: If you want to expand,
I shall see a cascade of stars
blessing your lovely form.*

*If you want to shrink,
I shall lay flowers at your feet.*

—Patricia Flasch—

IT FELT LOVE

How
Did the rose
Ever open its heart

And give to the world
All its
Beauty?

It felt the encouragement of light
Against its
Being,

Otherwise,
We all remain

Too
Frightened.

—Hafiz—

(Ladinsky, *The Gift: Poems by Haffiz*. Reprinted with permission.)

The Tyranny of Urgency

We recently had the opportunity to fulfill one of my husband David's dreams: to go to Hawaii with a small group of friends and family to celebrate his seventieth birthday. It was a glorious holiday and I felt nourished by the islands and the loved ones present. The experience has already become one of my fondest memories.

During David's birthday, while we were having champagne, we told many wonderful stories about David's life and the ways that he has touched us all. Then we created a wedding ceremony for my niece, Lori, and her partner, Jeannie, and supported their young, sweet love. It was awesome!

Vacationing on Maui amidst the tropical flowers, gentle ocean breezes, and sacred environment just added to the feeling of wonder and pleasure we created in sharing these two life events.

> Perhaps you can join with me in committing yourself to another way of approaching your life and work – 10% more peace and 10% less war inside. What do you say?

Returning from vacation allowed me to view my life anew.

The Tyranny of Urgency

Coming home from "hang loose" Hawaii highlighted the pace and urgency with which I live my life here in New Mexico. Over time I began to notice more of the underlying factors within me. I decided to write about my return to Santa Fe and the feelings it brought up. Many of my clients have shared with me that it's often a bumpy ride returning to work after a holiday. So, I thought I'd offer my perspective on what may be occurring.

Perhaps, sweet *love dogs*, you can relate to the lack of tenderness we often experience as we step from our times of respite and vacation back into the work world. It is the lack of tenderness for ourselves, really, that causes the problem. It's almost as if we have to make up for the time out by working harder prior to departure and harder still on return. This is a sad thing. It's my purpose here to point out how it feels when we enter urgency and take our puritan work ethic too seriously. If by writing this soul note I can save myself even 10% of hardness towards myself and I can save you that same 10%, I will be happy.

As you read along, if you can relate to this "tyranny of urgency" perhaps you can join with me in committing yourself to another way of approaching your life and work — 10% more peace and 10% less war inside. What do you say?

Shortly after my return to Santa Fe from Maui, I went to a Benedictine monastery to reflect on my inner experience. This writing is my journal account of those days. I end with a step-by-step process we can use to move away from the tyranny of urgency towards an experience of being in the moment, thriving in our lives, and treating ourselves more tenderly.

I invite you along, dear reader, on this journey. It is my heartfelt position that we can have a 10% increase in tenderness and away from the tyranny of urgency and still get the outcome we want. When we lighten our grip on ourselves we often, though not always, get surprisingly better results. I do *know*, beyond a shadow of a doubt, that when I am filled with tenderness and ease with myself—truly present—I allow my clients to relax into their most openhearted selves and our collaborative results are astounding. When *love dog* meets *love dog* within a session, communion takes place and the outcome takes care of itself.

Journal Entry – February 6, 2007
I have been exhausted ever since we returned from Hawaii and David's birthday party. The celebration and the times with friends and family were genuinely beautiful. Both David's birthday and my beloved niece's wedding ceremony were such sacred moments.

And, I came back truly tired. One part of this equation is that while my husband is energized by social interactions, and among the most outgoing human beings on the planet, I lean towards the introverted side. So the vacation fed me deeply in terms of relationships that really matter to me and I've been depleted. I could see that I really needed to take a time out for replenishment and rejuvenation.

So, I'm currently writing from the Benedictine Monastery Center nestled in the northern New Mexico mountains. I'm getting away to rest and write for three days. I so need this time of introspection—a time to tend only to my relationship with myself and to see what my heart wants to write.

Several weeks ago, one of my clients was talking to me about the tyranny of urgency and it stuck in my brain. I thought that the next time I write, I'll write about that. I want to explore how the tyranny of urgency works within me, for my own edification. In doing so, I hope to be of Service to you, my *love dog* readers.

So what is the tyranny of urgency? In one way, the tyranny of urgency is this feeling that I cannot hit the "pause" button. When I am in urgency it feels as if both my personal and professional lives are on the speed dial. I eat, speak, and move quickly. I'm like a locomotive flying down the tracks at breakneck speed completely forgetting the journey, focusing only on the destination. This urgency feeling is a kind of adrenalin addiction

The Tyranny of Urgency

How has this urgency fix played out in my life? I remember that twice in the last few years I've fallen flat on my face and dislocated first my right elbow, then my left. On the one hand, I tripped on a jagged rock and then the next time fell into an unmarked hole in the street in the dark. On the other hand, both times I was *not present*. I was hurrying. I was not really in my body on the walk. I was in my mind thinking and doing. I was not "being" on the hike. I was doing what my frightened mind is so used to doing: thinking and talking and rushing down the road.

> **The only place to create the possibility of safety is in our inner lives.**

I wonder where I'm going anyway. I wonder really what the rush is. Am I running away from the present moment? If so, why? Is there a deeper psychological issue? If so, what is it? Is this somehow related to my father's accidental and sudden death? It may be that the rushing started then. Maybe that was when I began to run away from my feelings. That might have been when I could not really tolerate the present moment. (Consider when the urgency began for you, dear reader.)

When I look around me, in my everyday world, I see lots of folks rushing right along side me. Sitting here by the window at the monastery, being present in the moment, and looking over the field that's just coming into spring, this urgency thing feels so false and meaningless. There is a lovely little pond here just outside the window. A momma duck and her seven babies floated by just before lunch. A little later it looked like there was a snake skimming across the surface of the pond, and, on closer look, I realized it was a beaver.

It's wonderful to be unplugged for a while. And I wonder, "Why don't I do this more?" After all, I am self-employed. I do get to choose my own schedule and have done so for decades. And to be fair, there are many times that I do unhook from rushing. Yet, right now my purpose is to reflect on all those times when I am living in the tyranny of urgency.

By the way, it's not that I'm meaning to blame myself here. It's rather that I want to come to know myself more deeply. In doing so, hopefully, I will give you a chance to look more clearly at the pacing in your own life and at the energy with which you fuel your own journey.

In exploring the phrase "the tyranny of urgency," I wonder: Is urgency really tyrannical? I often think of a tyrannical, abusive parent, or an extremist dictator. "Tyranny" is such a strong word. There is, though, a *tyrant* that lives in me and dictates large chunks of my personal and professional life. Is this also true for you, dear reader?

I'm thinking about the way our world is right now: in the midst of this tragic war with Iraq, teetering on a conflict with North Korea, facing global warming where the sweet polar bears can no longer swim long enough to be able to land on ice, where things are so out of balance that elephants are raping rhinos in Africa. Perhaps the elephants, who are losing the territory they need to survive, are terrorizing rhinos because they no longer feel safe.

Maybe that's it: the tyranny of urgency springs directly from our knowingness that we are not safe. Prior to 9/11, many of us thought we were safe, but now our growing spiritual and emotional maturity (in combination with a very messy world) shows us that safety does not really exist in the world today. The only place to create the possibility of safety is in our inner lives.

I remember in graduate school that one of my favorite books was *The Wisdom of Insecurity* by Alan Watts. Facing insecurity and allowing myself to come to know it, even then, felt much safer than pretending to be secure.

Insecurity, instability, and the tyranny of urgency are linked.

The Tyranny of Urgency

This outer world, as it stands, makes it quite challenging to try to create an inner world in which I can have visits with tranquility.

Another possibility is that I and "we" as a collective are running so fast because we are mortal. Perhaps rushing through the world is an attempt to avoid death. What is the purpose of that? We're all heading to the same place. We are dying as we speak and none of us are getting off this boat alive. I don't mean this in a gruesome sort of way. I mean it as a truth. Our bodies are mortal. Thinking that rushing around will save us somehow from the "grim reaper" is certainly not a spiritual truth.

I'm starting to get uncomfortable now about writing boldly about this broken place inside me. The magnitude of it seems embarrassing. After all, if we were to take a glimpse at my life—that I'm a Soul Whisperer with a thriving practice, a loving and loyal husband, surrounded by *love dog* friends, a wonderful lifestyle, good health, etc.—it doesn't make much sense that this urgency thing sits in the center of my experience as much of the time as it does. But it does and I want, more than saving face, to tell the truth because the truth, as you know, sets us free.

I'll hang in there with the urgency a little deeper, a little longer to see if I can tolerate its exposure. There are entire meals I've never tasted, entire cities I've driven through without noticing, lengthy conversations that I have completely missed.

There are so many driven moments that they add up to, to well what? To a life that sometimes feels empty of Presence, to sleepless nights, to agonizing moments, to unchecked neurosis, to spiritual and emotional bankruptcy.

Wow, what ever happened to my pause button? And, what may have happened to yours? Why fast food? Why not slow food? Why fast lane? Why do I need to get an "A" all the time? Are you a perfectionist as well? Why? Why am I so absolutely sure that what I *do* matters so much more than *who I am*? I don't really believe this to be true though I do live as if I believe it to be true. When

I stop and ask myself this last question, I know that it is not true that *doing* is more important than being. But my old, unexamined belief, that runs my life until I stop and question it, is that MY VERY SURVIVAL IS DEPENDENT ON DOING WHAT I DO PERFECTLY.

I believe that at the bottom of every single issue is the SURVIVAL issue. *Urgency* is our way of suppressing our feelings of fear and *urgency* is a way to act out the feelings that OUR VERY LIVES ARE IN DANGER.

One of the blessings of my work as a Soul Whisperer is that I get to share wisdom with my clients that I, too, need to hear. I'm thinking now of the countless clients who talk to me about their overwhelming "to do lists." First, I always respond that I do *know* what they mean. What we generally talk about next is that the "to do list" is killing us. Then we talk about how the "to do list" is eternal. It never stops. It will most likely still be happening on our deathbed as we sort out the will and check off all the folks we need to connect with before we die.

> **I have had countless experiences of going through my day with grace as my primary partner. On these days, my work is effortless. On these days I am breathing with the pulse of the Universe. On these days, I am just pleased to be alive in all my cells.**

Next we begin to collaborate about how the "to do list" has killed off the "to be list" when we were not even looking. We talk about whether there might be another way to "hold" this list. Perhaps there could be a party next New Year's Eve where people all over the world burn their "to do lists" and start experiencing their "to be lists." This would be the year we collectively decided that "not setting goals" is more important than "setting goals."

I'm not meaning to give "goal setting" a bad rap. It's an

important part of my personal and professional life. But, I believe I have (and maybe you have) gotten carried away with goal setting, this "I gotta get to the destination" thing.

In this moment, as a sixty-year-old woman, I wonder whether or not I want my remaining years to include a whole long list of accomplishments, and that's all, or whether I really want to live richly, in the present moment, with great tenderness for myself, fueled more by grace than adrenalin. If I want that—that experience of living from a place of grace more frequently—what would I need to do? (Notice the "do" orientation again.)

Well then, how would I need to be? Perhaps in the mornings when we do our prayers and meditation, I can ask for help to remain in the present moment. Most days I really do remember to give my day to Tenderness. I remind myself that it's not really ME doing this soul whispering with people. It's the *Ones I Hold Most Dear* working through me. I'm not a "sole" practitioner; I am a "soul" practitioner. Those days I remember to make myself a hollow flute for Tenderness are my personal High Holy Days.

If, just for today, I can remember to walk, not run, that's a blessing. If, just for today, I can remember to chew, that's a miracle. If, just for today, I can rest when I am being with people, and truly allow Tenderness to be the voice that speaks through me, then I can have communion with the *love dogs* who show up for sessions.

> **Imagine your most beloved friend on earth was feeling urgent and overwhelmed, how would you treat them? Offer yourself that same kindness.**

If, just for today, I can skip the "to do list," whew, that would really be playing hooky wouldn't it? Or maybe I can't (and you can't either) skip the "to do list" but at least we could hold it more lightly. We could hold it more like a tai chi dance than a boxing match.

I have had countless experiences of going through my day with grace as my primary partner. On these days, my work is effortless. On these days I am breathing with the pulse of the Universe. On these days, I am just pleased to be alive in all my cells.

There are days in my marriage when we push and rush and challenge each other to do more. Then we check in at the end of our day to see how much we accomplished. Those days we fight more. We rush and then we fight. Then there are days when we choose to slow down, pause, and speak more slowly and more softly to one another. We take the time to see the love shining in one another's eyes. Now those are the days that make the Spirit sing.

In the last few months we've instituted a new agreement where at the end of our day we talk at least as much about the times we paused or put the "to do" list down—the nap we took or the hike we enjoyed—as we talk about what we accomplished. We want to reinforce the idea that we are what we "be" more than what we "do." It's funny sometimes and it's challenging to consider an entirely new model. It's as if we have stepped away from the "American way." We have stepped into the great void just to give voice to our *beings*.

It gives me great joy to honor my husband, David, by encouraging him to play more Sudoku puzzles, watch more sports, taste more wine, rest more, and consciously help him build his inner sense of relaxation. And, I so love when he supports my *being*. We have such a long, long way to go to undo all this urgency business. However, we have come so very far, all of us, just by acknowledging how it fuels our daily lives, unconsciously and dominantly, and by recognizing the cost to our well-being. When we own this, it takes the wind out of urgency's sails.

A while ago we spent a four-day weekend in Taos, New Mexico. On our drive there we decided the greatest gift we could give one another was a *slow* weekend. So, we walked, talked, and

The Tyranny of Urgency

chewed slowly. It is astounding to me how much more content I feel with my spouse and myself when I slow down.

I spent many hours writing this book *slowly* and with a sense of profound peace. Here is another surprise: I was more productive, not less, as a result of slowing down.

I want to be careful that my mind does not take off in another of its favorite directions: "I'm bad when I have an urgency addiction," vs. "I'm good when I know I'm fueled by grace." This is really not a moral issue and there is no good girl/bad girl dance going on here. There is only this one sweet *love dog* soul looking inside to see what's happening, to share the unabashed joy that comes from honest, innocent, self-reflection.

Do I want to move more towards fueling my life with grace and further away from fueling my life with urgency? Absolutely. Do I want to make myself wrong for all my urgent cries? *Absolutely Not!* Nor do I want to be urgent about addressing these urgency issues.

I just want to notice, and I want to encourage you to notice, both the urgency and the fact that we do have choice around urgency. Here's an idea—rather than trying to finish this chapter before dinner—I'll take a break. I can pick it up where I left off. That would give me time for a rest and some moments to read a chapter of my romance novel.

I promise myself to walk slowly into the dinner hall tonight, to be present as I eat my silent meal with these Benedictine brothers and sisters. I promise to chew. I promise to take at least three big breaths before I close up this laptop computer and go out to dinner. Thanks for listening. By the way, if I forget my promises, I promise to forgive myself and go back to my present moment and the slower pace.

When I return I'd like to talk about how we can make that shift towards grace (or whatever your favorite holy word is) and away from urgency.

Well, I took a longer break from this writing than I'd planned. What a wondrous thing. I went back to the pond. I listened to the monks chanting their evening lauds. I noticed over the dinner hour last night that only one monk went back for seconds. When I eat in moderation and I chew I don't need seconds either. That's a blessing.

Last night I also spent my time giving myself some room to grieve about my dying dog and my ill husband, just to be in tenderness with myself and write for my own personal enrichment. This was a small celebration of leaning further into just being.

> **Remember that it's truly possible to teach ourselves a way of being that is centered on the present moment and not on our old hypervigilant ways.**

I'm so glad I gave myself this gift of time away for myself. I will encourage others to do the same when it is appropriate. When a loved one is ill, especially if it is over an extended period of time, it is essential that the caregiver take care of himself or herself. Coming to a monastery is just one of the many, many possibilities for self-care.

This morning I see that there are really only a few more remaining things to say. It would be helpful to share more about how we can move further away from the tyranny of urgency and closer to being in the moment. Remember now, you too have wonderful wisdom available within and I too have a very human condition. I am an equal soul friend on the journey with you.

Clues on relaxing into being a *love dog*, moving from urgency to tenderness:
- Noticing that we are in urgency—that we are gripping the phone or pushing the gas pedal too hard—is the first step. It's important to notice from a position of curiosity and tenderness rather than self-judgment.

- Do not suppress the feelings. Allow yourself to have the feelings. "Wow, I see I'm frantic here and my pulse is fast and my breath is shallow. What's happening in me? I'm frightened and I've got my adrenalin pumping."
- Do not exaggerate the feelings. No need to dramatize. When we suppress our feelings, they get bigger. When we exaggerate our feelings, they also get bigger. Just simply have the feelings.
- Do honor your feelings. Do speak to yourself sweetly. Do make room inside to be a human being who is having some moments of the tyranny of urgency. Do allow yourself to feel the fear, the frantic energy, and the hidden sorrow, whatever it is.
- Do bless yourself in the midst of your feelings. Kiss yourself on the forehead in your mind's eye. Imagine your most beloved friend on earth was feeling urgent and overwhelmed, how would you treat them? Offer yourself that same kindness.
- Do consider an action that may break the spell. For example, you could let go of your grip on the phone, or the "to do" list. You could take your foot off the gas. You could pause and take a few deep breaths. You could remind yourself that even if you are late or you don't get something done, it truly is not the end of the world. It's an opportunity to forgive yourself and it's a place to prioritize your pace over your outcome. The funny thing is, most of the time when I relax and slow down, I notice that my outcomes happen anyway. They just happen with ease rather than push.

Remember that it's truly possible to teach ourselves a way of being that is centered on the present moment and not on our old hypervigilant ways. Any meditation practice will help us return to the now moment. Neelam, a spiritual teacher in Sri Ramana Maharshi's lineage, says, "Tenderness is not something you add to your life, it is something that you uncover." Let's join together in uncovering those sweet moments of tenderness that are available to us today.

> When she stopped rushing
> through life
> she was amazed
> how much more life
> she had time for.
>
> —Amy Rubin—

> When you do things from your soul
> you feel a river moving in you,
> a joy.
>
> When action comes from another section,
> the feeling disappears.
>
> —Rumi—
>
> (Barks, *The Soul of Rumi: A New Collection of Ecstatic Poems*, p.79. Reprinted with permission)

Effort vs. Inspiration

In my private practice as a Soul Whisperer and business catalyst, I work with countless clients every week who try very hard to get the results they want in their lives and businesses. This trying often turns into a kind of drivenness and then the life force seeps out of what it is they were doing. They lose a sense of purpose, lose the spring in their step and start to experience a variety of difficult emotions.

All of these folks, without exception, have wonderful intentions. But, the way they are going about trying to make things happen is causing suffering.

I know there is a way where we can hold our to do list more lightly and still get the outcomes we want. If we hold the list with tenderness and devotion—and we stop holding it with angst and drive—we still often do get where we want to go, but we get there without trampling on our own hearts along the way.

When we fuel our work with a pushy kind of EFFORT, we often step away from working with grace and tenderness as our ally. We think we get more done by pushing, when in reality, we cause ourselves more suffering along the way. We step away from being *love dogs*.

Effort vs. Inspiration

James Loehr and Tony Schwartz teach us to be involved in work for time frames that inspire us (Loehr and Schwartz, *The Power of Full Engagement*). They encourage ninety-minute work intensives, followed by thirty-minute breaks. They teach us to work from a position of spiritual, emotional and physical balance rather than the old pedal to the metal approach.

> **Whatever you are experiencing emotionally this now moment and throughout the rest of your days, please consider the coaching paradigm that 'nobody gets to be wrong.' Your feelings can live in an honorable place inside your own being.**

In this soul note I offer you a window into a process of my own that often occurs before I present a workshop. You will witness how it is for me when I am wearing my "we try harder" button. You will journey with me as I move towards the thoughts that make me try so hard. Once I have expressed the forceful approach, an alchemical shift begins and I naturally move towards an approach that is easy, fluid, and heart opening. Ultimately, I surrender to grace and allow the results to unfold. I close this soul note with a few words of caution based on my experience using the Law of Attraction to manifest what I want in my life.

It's exciting to discover that we can step away from "drive" and into the arms of "ease." We can stop pushing at any moment in time and, as we do so, miracles can occur.

When we are able to forgive, release and transform our memory bodies (the back seats of our vehicles of self-compassion) what remains is our inspiration. The root of the word inspiration is the Latin *in* and *spirare* (breathe), or in other words, to breathe into. When we get out of the way, it is Spirit that breathes into us. We join with Spirit to produce our results.

Thank you for joining me on this discovery process. Please

remember, as with all the other soul notes, our feelings are our friends and they often provide powerful messages for our souls. Whatever you are experiencing emotionally this now moment and throughout the rest of your days, please consider the coaching paradigm that *nobody gets to be wrong*. Your feelings can live in an honorable place inside your own being. When you have made space inside for a full range of feelings, you are well on your way to *becoming a love dog*.

Forcing the Outcome
I'm writing this soul note five days before giving a workshop called *The Money Dance/Exploring the True Richness of our Lives,* part of a series on *Leaving Your Patterns Not Your Partners.*

I've created and facilitated more than five hundred personal growth workshops over the past thirty-five years and every one begins with my own inner journey. So, I spent my early hours this morning experiencing a great grief cry. I surrendered to the disappointment, discouragement and despair that are holding court deep within my being today.

The thing is, the results for the workshop are not what I had hoped. The enrollment process has been going poorly. My intended outcome was thirty to forty participants. The actual outcome will be between twelve and sixteen participants (unless the Universe has a surprise climax in mind).

I am so utterly attached to getting the results I WANT. I am efforting beyond belief; it's a bit as if I'm walking up a mountain, naked, with a ton of bricks on my back, in winter. Perhaps this is a bit of an exaggeration. You get my drift though.

While I was sharing my feelings about the seminar with my beloved husband this morning, I began to notice a much larger grief. I have been in the coaching/counseling field for thirty-five years. During that time I estimate I have offered approximately 250,000 personal invitations to workshops, seminars, private work, and retreats.

Effort vs. Inspiration

I began to notice how it's felt to receive perhaps 235,000 *no's*. As much as I would like to be a woman who can invite with my whole heart and then let go of the result completely, I am only that about 70% of the time. The other 30% of the time I am completely caught up in the outcome.

I don't know how much that comes across with students because, on the outer, I have become more and more skillful at allowing their response to be held in a sacred way. So, today, when they say, *no,* I treat them honorably and accept their decision with as much kindness as I can muster.

And, on the inside, I am often hurt, sad, mad and, on occasion—tormented. Whew, what a powerful word, tormented. The little one inside is totally convinced that every *no* means she's not good enough. She feels like so many people are saying, "*No,* I don't like you! *No,* I don't want to come to your party." She is genuinely devastated. As far as little Patti is concerned it's all about her—every *yes* and every *no*.

The adult and the one who is connected with the Great Silence, has a larger knowingness. She says, "Sweet woman, these results do not mean anything about you.

You, my dear one, remain in the lap of Tenderness no matter who comes and who goes in your life. Every *no* is leading us to a *yes.*"

When the little one grabs the wheel, it's painful, deeply painful. Little Patti can be inconsolable. She wreaks havoc in the middle of my belly. It takes some doing on my part to see if I can move her from inside my belly out on to my lap where the possibility of reparenting her is much more likely.

The next thing that often happens is that I begin to criticize my difficult emotions from my back seat.[*] I begin to shame myself for being so attached to the outcome. How can I possibly lead a

---

[*] See the soul note, "The Vehicle of Self-Compassion" for details on the back seat.

workshop that is about "letting go of your patterns" and "exploring the larger richness in our lives" and then grovel, beg and demand that I get it my way? I'm a fraud.

When I go deeply into self-criticism, as I have here, it's often as if a little tiny light bulb goes on. I've really allowed for the feelings and expressed the intensity of my discontent. My friend Amba calls this "bottoming out." I've taken the criticism far enough to allow the voice to express itself completely and I begin to pop out of it. My Observer kicks in, on some level, and begins to say, "Let's look at a larger picture."

So then, a place inside opens up where I am considering the possibility of what's really going on with me. Perhaps this hurt and anger, this concern about results IS my workshop—just another dimension of *my workshop*.

Perhaps this *forcing the outcome* is what my learning in preparation for the seminar really *is*. This grief about the 250,000 invitations and all of those *no's* is a part of my healing. Behind the sadness and all the mini-losses I've faced is a growing understanding of what this is all about.

My family was in the lower income bracket, at least after my father's death. What has been the pusher/fueler of many of the invitations is my *survival need*. Along with the character that needs to survive is another character that doesn't trust the Universe. I have lived with the feeling that "I have to make it on my own" since I was seven years old. I have fought hard and tried harder than just about anyone I know. I became my own parent very early in my life. That struggle for survival shows up as a cellular memory that is asking for attention and healing each time I step further into the world and ask for the results I want.

> **Our outer world does not determine our inside story.**
> **Rather, our inner world determines our outside story.**

Again, I want to make this part wrong. It's wrong to have

Effort vs. Inspiration

tried so hard and pulled so many folks in. That old world male inside me is a *bad guy. We need to kill him off.*

Or is he a *bad guy?* Maybe he's just a guy and maybe my need to survive is holy. Maybe the gas I've used all this time was the gas I needed to use to get my car down the road. (This thought is the beginning of emotional integration)

I'd like to ask you, my *love dog* reader, to pause a moment to ask some inner questions. Where is it in your own life that you have most pushed the outcome? How has it felt? When you are trying so hard to MAKE IT HAPPEN, whatever 'it' is, how do you experience your life? When you know that you are pushing and using adrenalin to create your results, how does that feel in your soul?

Thank God we decided to offer this workshop, as it is the vehicle that is showing me how much denial I've had about my "efforting." It is giving me a felt sense of what forcing the outcome is all about and where it comes from within.

As an aside, the reality is I have really achieved wonderful results in the course of my business. I have lived and traveled well. I have always been able to do what feels right for me to do. I live a very blessed and simply abundant life.

In fact, the financial results of this workshop don't matter much in my world. I have a really thriving private practice and create a wonderful level of financial reserves every single month. The 15,000 *yes's* have been the foundation for a life with a great deal of financial ease at its center.

So then this grief cry is not about my actual overall *reality*. It is about healing the pattern. In this case the pattern is forcing the outcome.

I'm not sharing the success of my professional life as an attempt to deny the grief process. Rather, I am sharing the actual results in my world to demonstrate that the outside picture doesn't really matter. I have had millionaires tell me, with total candor, they cannot afford a weekend seminar *and* a few welfare participants say they'll do whatever it takes to create their participation.

Our outer world does not determine our inside story. Rather, our inner world determines our outside story. And, there is a much larger picture that I'll talk about before closing this soul note.

Though my back seat characters are all lined up with the goal—the outcome, the way it *should* look—they are not the voices for truth, they are the voices for my human condition and my old wounding. The fact that they say, "We lost, we're failing, we can't do it, we're not doing it right, the Universe doesn't support us, we're a miserable excuse for a personal growth teacher," *does not make it true!*

Looking deeper we see the voices all come from a very human place. We all have that core need for survival and we all have a "doubting Thomas" that lives somewhere inside the vast cavern of our psyche.

Here's where it begins to get exciting. If my survival need is not *wrong* and I can kiss my fingertips for all the times I have clawed my way to my result, *then*, maybe we're talking about something else entirely.

Shifting from Effort to Inspiration

When I look for the positive intention behind my various stages of grief, I see something beautiful. The positive intention behind every single workshop was my own desire for profound healing. What has always been beneath this worldly dance is my sincere calling towards spiritual transformation, beginning with myself and then passing it on. I do these workshops, all of them, because they inspire my own healing and then they open a space within me that operates as a very authentic and tender channel for all the participants. I have never been able to skip the part about the healing that takes place in me on my way to the workshop. How fortunate is that?

Effort vs. Inspiration

I recently completed a workshop facilitated by Isabel Parlett entitled *The True Spirit of Your Work.*** The purpose statement that I arrived at during the workshop was this: *The true spirit of my work is to gather together the most willing souls on earth (the* love dogs*) into a partnership of truth and tenderness so that they can leave their caves, stand in all their glory, and celebrate with their tribe."*

That is the face of my truest intention and has always been what I am really about and what my heart most wants to offer.

I repeat, the journey always begins within.

So, while I set a loose intention to offer this workshop to twenty or more participants in mid September at Santa Fe Soul, I always say, "*This or something greater.*" Most of the time, in the most human part of me, I mean, "THIS AND ONLY THIS BECAUSE I KNOW WHAT IS BEST FOR ME." It's only offering lip service to God to say, "This or something better."

At its core, the something *better* is the redemption of my own soul. My capacity to discover yet another older, deeper, darker pattern and find a way to hold it in tenderness for myself so that I can "leave the cave, stand in all my glory, and celebrate with my tribe" is what really matters.

It turns out that what is important is not how many people come to the next workshop or what those results look like in the world. It's to welcome those willing *love dogs* who do come, and offer the healing from my purpose statement, hand in hand with each participant's own purpose statement.

Discovering Purpose

Remembering my purpose has played an essential part in helping me to shift from trying to force a specific workshop outcome. Some of you may be thinking, "I don't have a purpose," or wondering, "How can I find my purpose?" Discovering your personal purpose

---

** For more on Isabel's excellent work on tapping the power of language, go to her website at www.parlancetraining.com

can be as simple as beginning to ask yourself questions like: "What is my purpose today?" "What is my purpose for this trip?" "What is my purpose for this business meeting or family gathering?" As we become familiar with our purpose in simple, everyday situations, we often begin to discover a theme, an inner knowingness, about what really matters to us.

Another great way to discover your purpose is an idea from Julia Cameron (Cameron, V*ein of Gold)*. She suggests that we list our five favorite movies of all time and then figure out what the primary theme or the main attraction is that draws us to each of those movies. This central theme is a clue for our own purpose.

> **This is when work feels like worship.**

Knowing our purpose and remembering it daily is one of the ways we can shift from "effort to inspiration." My simple purpose, "To reveal the presence of grace," in and of itself, when I am deeply connected with it, doesn't encourage effort or force. It encourages me to breathe with ease.

A practice that I've been using for years as part of my morning meditation is to sit and hold gently in my hands the list of things I'll be doing during the day and the list of clients I'll be seeing. I imagine myself, in each situation, really resonating with my purpose statement. I imagine sitting with my morning clients and feeling truly centered in the idea of "revealing the presence of grace." I imagine relaxing my voice, easing my breath, seeing if there is one simple contribution that I could make to help the client experience an aspect of authenticity, direction or compassion. I see grace landing in their laps. I see them noticing the path of the *love dog* opening before them.

Then I imagine myself later in the day working on the computer: writing, editing, and feeling utterly present. I imagine that the words flow out of me like the river Rumi speaks of in the

Effort vs. Inspiration

opening quote. This is when work feels like worship.

This is what it means to "set" my day so that I allow inspiration to flow in my life. I use my purpose statement as the focus and impetus to come from this tender place.

When we set our intention motivated by a driven one and coming from the back seat of our unresolved conditioning, we may or we may not get what we say we want. If it comes from our conditioning though, we won't be satisfied. We'll just keep calling out MORE! MORE! MORE!

Soul satisfaction comes from allowing the process to unfold through our heartbreaking humanity into our true *spirit*.

> **May the whole world, without exception, be free from fear and deeply comforted!**

Maybe that partnership you say you want is not what's best for you. Maybe it's your marriage to yourself that really matters, or your relationship to emptiness. The value of your soul does not show up on a bank statement *and* we do want and need to take care of ourselves in the physical world as best we can. Not one or the other, but both.

I'm not saying, don't set intentions or care about goals. I am saying take it deeper. Inner fulfillment comes from taking it deeper to discover what it is that *really* matters to you. Once you have the inner fulfillment, what is truly best naturally emerges.

In my mind, it's wonderful if we get our desired result. If we don't get our desired result, it's wonderful in a whole other way. (We get soul healing and we grow in compassion for ourselves. My husband David reminds me of Lance Armstrong's recent book, *It's Not About the Bike*.) Well, it's not about the results either.

I'd like to close this section with a letter of surrender to my higher power:

Becoming a Love Dog

Dear Tenderness (my sweet teacher of truth):

I know you've been with me today through the great grief cry and the falling on my knees. Thank you for taking me there and meeting me there.

I do place the outcome of this seminar in your holy hands.

You know how I get carried away by the numbers and what I think they mean about me. Show me please, how to love the one within who tries so hard.

And, I now release the remaining results for this weekend workshop into your lap. The numbers are up to you.

Just keep me close to my true spirit statement.

Thank you for showing me these unresolved aspects of myself. Keep showing me how to bless them.

I ask that all the folks who said yes *and all the folks who said* no *to this particular seminar receive the results of a clearer "Money Dance" and a deeper richness in their overall lives.*

I agree to participate with all of my being and ask that I be a flute for your words. Sing your songs through me. I am your servant.

May the whole world, without exception, be free from fear and deeply comforted!

Love, Patricia, Patti and all my inner voices.

Today, after yesterday's meltdown, and with a tremendous sense of forgiveness for myself and all my old and wounded parts, *Tenderness* is now, once again, driving my car.

Today I am happy to have the workshop look and feel and be whatever it's meant to be. I am delighted to welcome the *love dogs* who arrive on Friday evening and feel blessed to offer the material that comes through this flute on the topic of money and true richness.

My own life is richer for the process yesterday. I feel closer to my spouse for his care and listening. I feel closer to my two soul friends, Amba and Chittak, who were sweet and kind in listening

Effort vs. Inspiration

to my soul story. I feel that the inner bond with Tenderness and the bond with my soul friends have shifted into another layer of depth.

Later today, when I make my follow up calls to the remaining folks on the list who have expressed interest but not yet decided about their participation in the workshop, I am quite sure that I can offer the invitation wholeheartedly, with no hooks, *and* that I can let go effortlessly if they say, *no*. I am, once again, inspired to make those calls.

That sense of feeling "driven" has shifted and the openness for creation has taken its place.

I have no emotional charge about the outcome and I am genuinely excited about the workshop. At this point in time I am feeling so blessed to be able to offer the work that comes through me that I would do the workshop if my husband and I were the only participants. Yesterday's meltdown itself, as much as the working through it and the rising from it, feels incredibly valuable. The personal evolution that needed to take place for me has been completed and now I'm ready to make my offering. I can hold a genuinely open hearted space for the *love dog* participants.

I have a sense that this material about *effort vs. inspiration* will be an essential part of the workshop.

It is now six months after completing the Money Dance workshop. The results of the September 2006 workshop were that twenty people participated. It was one of the most powerful workshops I've ever offered or attended. Months later we are still receiving gratitude from participants about how it turned their lives around.

The participants came from such an openhearted place—with such a willingness to shift their thinking about themselves and to forgive themselves—that I believe a miracle happened for all of us. I believe that workshop will impact all of our lives, both financially and emotionally, for years to come.

Working with the Law of Attraction

As I write this soul note, much of the personal growth world, at least those people most interested in prosperity, are focusing on *The Secret**** and the work of Esther and Jerry Hicks: The Teachings of Abraham****. Though different in a number of ways, both bodies of work deal with the Law of Attraction—we attract into our lives what we focus on. We can consciously work toward getting what we want by using the Law of Attraction. I would like to close this writing about "Effort vs. Inspiration" with a few words on using the Law of Attraction.

For many, many years I studied the "thought is creative" material and worked with teachers who believed that you simply need to put your intention out into the Universe, in complete clarity, then watch the results unfold. I often felt "less than" or ashamed if I could not seem to create what I said I wanted. I used the idea of "taking responsibility" as an opportunity to beat myself up.

I remember one teacher telling me that all you had to do to know what you want is look at your results. I took that to mean that when my results didn't mesh with my desires, I failed. I was unconsciously using personal growth teachings to continue my "back seat" story that said, "There must be something wrong with me."

Just recently, as Oprah discussed *The Secret* on two separate TV shows, I see a similar teaching emerging. It genuinely concerns me that many of the folks in the audience will use the information from *The Secret* to implode—to shame and blame themselves for the results they are currently getting.

The Secret offers what I believe is one of the truths in the

....

*** *The Secret*, a video seminar on DVD directed by Drew Heriot, © TS Production, LLC, 2006

**** For example, *Introducing Abraham - The Secret Behind "The Secret"* a video seminar on DVD, with Esther and Jerry Hicks, © Hay House, 2007

Effort vs. Inspiration

Universe: that there is a Law of Attraction—that what we think, we feel, and then we manifest. What we think most about we create more of. If we want to shift our results we can think more about what we truly want.

> I want to remind us all that there are no "good" or "bad" feelings or "good" or "bad" experiences. Any feeling that is truly welcomed is a "good" feeling. Any experience that we learn from is a "good" experience. Supporting duality-thinking causes suffering.

I have experienced how the Law of Attraction works thousands of times. Just recently we decided we wanted to buy a newer car. We wanted the car to offer great gas mileage, to be one of the pastel colors, to have an impeccable and state-of-the-art interior and exterior, to be in sound mechanical condition and to be priced under $10,000. It seemed a pretty tall order.

The honest truth is we had the discussion at home about what we really wanted and drove onto the first car dealership and found the car. The sticker price for the car was $13,500 and my husband, because the dealership had misrepresented the car's background, was able to get the car for $6,500 and we spent an additional $600 on repairs. It's such a beauty. It even has leather seats that warm up for winter driving.

Voila! The Law of Attraction worked.

But, what about what happens when we say we want "perfect health" and then we discover a tumor? See, how easy it is to go from, "I created this" to, "It's my fault." In this case, the Law of Attraction becomes a whip with which to beat ourselves. If instead, we can pause and forgive ourselves for our heartbreaking humanity, for the places in our bodies that are less than perfect, for all aspects of our human condition, we can progress in a softer, gentler way. We can begin affirming, "I am open to my own healing." "I see my financial picture clearing up." "All my relationships are coming into harmony."

If we can apply true tenderness to that tumor, or that divorce, or that extra twenty pounds—if we can find room in our hearts for it, even to bless it—then we can move towards opening up our health, relationship, or financial picture. We cannot deny where we are now. If we blame and shame ourselves that blame and shame will only exacerbate what we are experiencing. Also, because we are mortal, perhaps that tumor is a part of our destiny and it is our "time." Not because we've failed but because it is "what is." Rather than feeling responsible for it, perhaps we are responsible to it.

I want to remind us all that there are no "good" or "bad" feelings or "good" or "bad" experiences. Any feeling that is truly welcomed is a "good" feeling. Any experience that we learn from is a "good" experience. Supporting duality-thinking causes suffering. Opening to our authentic experience breeds aliveness. Aliveness opens our possibilities. The more alive, vibrant and passionate we are, the more we are capable of drawing what we want towards us.

The Secret has a powerful message *and* there is a bigger picture. Today, when I look in my world I see a glorious manifestation of my true desires and I am so pleased. *And*, I see places of brokenness and sorrow; places that make my rough stone smooth. I am so grateful. I really don't want a life that cuts away the journey to the soul. I stand for the whole range of human expression and coming to know my "back seat characters" as my dearest friends. That's the way this *love dog* sees the world.

This new feeling of "allowance" creates an internal experience of peace and connectedness. This emotional/spiritual integration place is more valuable than any result in the world. And, it's totally okay to set goals and go for what we want in the world as long as

Effort vs. Inspiration

we remember, "This or something greater, for the greatest good of all concerned." The something "greater" may look quite different than what we had in mind.

Let's leave space for the unknown, for our destiny, and to allow the mystery to unfold.

Since you have made it to the end of this soul note, I assume that you have been struggling, on some level, with the topic, that you sometimes try hard to force an outcome and you are aware of your suffering when you push yourself.

My heart goes out to you and I so appreciate your willingness to consider a new paradigm, to take a breath, to trust a larger picture, to reflect on the possibility that the Universe wants you to have what you want, and that your desire can unfold with ease. Perhaps you can begin an experiment. Perhaps you can hold your "to do" list more gently and find inspiration that comes from a place in your heart of hearts.

Please remember that judging yourself when you notice that you have been coming from effort rather than inspiration will only cause more angst. Instead consider forgiving all the times you have tried so very hard, including this one, and then let go into the Great Silence. Continue taking strides toward your desired outcome, but take them with a light step.

All honor to you in your journey moving from effort to inspiration.

> Hurry hinders holiness.
>
> —Susan Rush—

> May only goodness and mercy follow you all the
> days of your life.
>
> Adapted from Psalm 23:6: "Surely goodness and mercy shall
> follow me all the days of my life"

> We are not responsible for our illness.
> We are responsible TO our illness.
> The question is not what did we do wrong,
> but rather,
> how can we take care of ourselves right now.
>
> —Stephen Levine—

Being Kind to Yourself When Ill

I have noticed both on my own life journey and in the lives of the *love dog* clients I work with on a daily basis that when we get sick we often experience emotional pain right along side the illness.

We live in a culture that berates illness and exonerates wellness. We receive thousands of ongoing messages that "death is bad" and "life is good." Unlike some eastern countries where the cultural belief is that dying is an honor and a natural part of the life cycle; we are death "phobic", we fight with death. Thus illness, death's precursor, gets a bad rap. These cultural messages are okay when we are feeling well and thriving. They are incredibly painful and counterproductive to our actual healing process when we are ill or we enter our dying process.

When we are ill, our own compassion and self-acceptance can be elemental aspects in the promotion of healing. When we are sick and then begin to berate ourselves and question ourselves—to emotionally poke ourselves with sharp sticks—the environment we create is a kind of toxic healing room.

Being ill and then emotionally beating ourselves up is a kind of double whammy. This soul note suggests another way of speaking to ourselves, a whole other way of being with ourselves, when we are sick. Let's call this the *love dog path* of being with ourselves when we are ill.

I invite you to consider a compassionate way to hold illness and the aging and dying process. We can work together to develop an internal dialogue that is kind, clear and powerful. Toward this end, I include in this soul note a step-by-step exercise to help heal self-rejection around illness.

You might ask how Being Kind to Yourself when Ill relates to *Becoming a Love Dog*? Having been professionally engaged as a psycho-spiritual counselor for more than thirty-five years, I realize that most people think the worst thing that can happen to them is to be alone. This happens either by losing their life partner through death or divorce, or by never finding a true mate. That's not what I believe to be true. *The worst thing that can happen is that we abandon or divorce ourselves.* You see, we sometimes unconsciously and sometimes consciously and intentionally refuse to be with ourselves. We are our own "fair weather" friends. *Unless* we are doing well physically, mentally, financially, and so on, we emotionally leave ourselves. We criticize and abuse ourselves.

This chapter is an invitation to release the pattern of self-rejection during illness. Let's begin today by honoring all the "less than perfect" parts of self.

Journal Entry - April 24, 2007

It's about 4:30 in the morning and I've been up for about an hour struggling with the symptoms of a cold—stuffy head, an aching around the eyes, clogged sinuses, and a sore throat. The "struggle" has lightened, however, because I've turned a corner in my process in the morning's wee hours.

For most of my life my approach to any illness or injury has been the following:

What have I done wrong to bring on this illness?
What can I do to fight it off?

What is wrong with my body?

How can I push through this?

How can I ignore my symptoms and go on with my life and work as if they are not present?

How can I fix it?

(*These are not* love dog *questions!*)

> **How can we meet this illness and care for ourselves with mercy? The merciful approach holds so much more capacity for healing than the Hitlerian approach.**

I have been fueling most illnesses and injuries with urgency and a genuine lack of tenderness towards myself. A few decades ago I learned from the new age movement that "thought is creative," meaning that I am totally responsible for what happens to me. I turned that new information into an opportunity to blame myself. I asked, "How can I take responsibility for this cold?" What I really meant was, "It's my fault and I have to fix it." Every illness or injury has been met by the powerful voice of my internal critic.

I see now that criticizing or blaming ourselves for an illness is truly counterproductive. How can our sweet bodies heal when our minds are waging war against ourselves? Think of it this way: imagine you are resting and recovering from an illness and another person walks into your bedroom and begins flinging insults at you, shouting at you, telling you it's your fault that you are sick. How would your body and mind respond to the verbal abuse? This is often the way we treat ourselves when we are ill. It's hard, if not impossible, to heal while the internal critic is assaulting us.

One of my favorite teachers of all time, Stephen Levine, says we are not, absolutely not, responsible for our illness; rather, we are responsible *to* it. In other words, the question is not "How did we create this?" The better question is "How can we meet this illness and care for ourselves with mercy?" The merciful approach holds so much more capacity for healing than the Hitlerian approach.

What's new this time is that my inner perspective about being ill has truly shifted. My initial thoughts when I felt the cold coming on were simply "How can I take care of myself?" I've taken some simple actions like getting herbs from the health food store, hydrating myself more, getting some vitamin C, and making some chicken soup.

The larger shift, though, is in how I am communicating with myself. I've been saying, "Well, if my body needs this cold, then I surrender." Perhaps I need a respite, a rest, a bit of a "time out" from my life and a "time in" to nurture myself within.

I've been saying to my inner little one, sweet Patti, that I love her and honor her and promise to take care of her completely during this cold. I've been reminding her that she's not a "bad girl" in any way at all. We don't even believe in the dualistic idea of "good and bad" anymore. She is a holy, innocent child of God. I have been bringing this little girl into my arms and into my heart. I have been kissing her on the forehead and reassuring her throughout the night.

One of my favorite biblical teachings is "You are my beloved daughter in whom I am well pleased." This bold statement Christ made was unequivocal, unconditional. There was not parenthesis (I love you and cherish you BUT...) He wasn't saying that love has exceptions. He was saying, "I love you when you are sick or dying or having an emotionally devastating time. I love you in your darkest hour." This example, by the way, is not meant to promote Christianity per se, but rather just to express one of Christ's teachings that may help deepen our understanding and our sense of compassion for ourselves in the midst of our suffering. *All spiritual paths are respected here, including agnosticism and atheism.*

Another of my favorite teachings of Christ was his message from the Garden of Gethsemane. I will always remember those early images I saw, on "holy cards" we purchased from the Catholic Church gift shop, of His leaning against a rock in the garden. His holy words, "Llama, llama, sabbathini"—roughly translated to mean, "My God, my God, why have you forsaken me?"—were the cry of the most vulnerable moment in his human life.

He showed us that He, too, doubted God's love for him when he was going through profound difficulty. When my struggles are deep, I automatically doubt the love God has for me, too. I have often thought that if I am in a profound struggle physically or emotionally, then God has dropped my hand.

The outcome of Christ's deep vulnerability near the rock and on the cross was his resurrection. That's true for each of us. When we surrender to the depths of our humanity, an alchemical shift occurs, and we are then resting in the arms of our Beloved.

I think Buddha's message by the Bodhi tree was similar though I don't know as much about the Buddha's story. I do know that Buddha said that "Life is Suffering" and that means that when we surrender to our suffering, we are on our "way home."

My clear picture in these wee hours is that God has never dropped my hand. I drop God's hand when I assume I've been abandoned. As soon as I "wake up," I see that it's my connection with the still calm voice deep inside that always partners me through every difficulty. There is an invisible hand holding me through life's great difficulties. I am standing in a circle joining hearts and hands with countless other *love dogs* I have never even met!

There are actually also many "visible" hands that hold me. I have dear friends, a sweet husband, and a giant spiritual and emotional support system. My life is lived in ongoing sanctuary provided by the ones I love and who love me. There is no one in my network, not one person, who would judge me for any part of a physical or emotional or spiritual challenge. All my best people care for me with ongoing mercy. I believe that my own

Being Kind to Yourself When Ill

growing mercy for myself has attracted this kind of unconditional love network.

To be honest, a part of me is embarrassed about the content of this writing. A part of me is buzzing in the background of my brain with the thought, "It's only a common cold. What the hell will you do when you get cancer or go into your dying process?" The internal critic, so it seems, always needs to have a voice. (My heart goes out to any of you reading this chapter who are facing serious illness. I am so sorry for your pain. I love you soul to soul!)

Here is my merciful response to this critic. "This cold is an opportunity to learn tenderness. It is also an opportunity to practice dying. If we can be kind to ourselves in the midst of a cold, we can build the muscle of mercy. It's good to start small. As we age, there will most likely be much larger challenges and this, sweet woman, is one small way to lift the old pattern of self-rejection and set out on a new path."

(In retrospect and for accuracy's sake, I want to say this "common cold" turned into a viral infection, a flu, and a period of very low energy that lasted two and a half months. So I had lots more practice using all these skills. There were days my husband had to feed me, days I crawled to the bathroom, whole nights without sleep, and many days I could not work, which is a very unusual experience for me).

As the night has gone on, I've been reviewing many of the times in the past where I was not tender with myself in illness or injury. I've been reminding myself to forgive myself for all past illnesses and injuries and all the times I have been clueless in the kindness department. I've spent some time doing my *Ho'oponopono* practice. *Ho'oponopono* has taught me to say to myself, to the thoughts and memories, "Dear ones, I am so sorry for all your past suffering and I love you very much."

Ho'oponopono, Patti, I'm so sorry for all your suffering and the memories replaying about having so many dental problems. I am so sorry that you were so badly judged because of the big gaps in your teeth. I am so sorry for all the suffering that went on regarding your teeth. And, I love you, very, very much.

Ho'oponopono, Patti, I am so sorry for all the emotional pain you experienced when your father, sister, grandparents and mother died, and all the times those memories have replayed. I am so very sorry and I love you so much.

Ho'oponopono, Patti, I am so sorry for the long year we spent having iritis and truly judging our poor dear eye for its weakness. I am so very sorry and I love you so much. Please forgive me.

Ho'oponopono, Patti, I am so sorry for all the physical pain we had when we dislocated one elbow and then the second elbow. I am sorry for the physical pain and the emotional pain we suffered back then from beating ourselves up. And, I love you so very much.

Ho'oponopono, Patricia, I am so sorry for a lifetime of physical and emotional problems that became places of despair and self-recrimination. I am so very, very sorry that I did not know how to cherish myself during those times. I am truly sorry. I love you today, this now moment, without condition.

I bless your stuffy head, sore sinuses, itchy throat and low energy. I am kissing you on the forehead now and caressing your sweet face. You do not have to change one hair on your head to be lovable. I kiss all the old memories replaying that say it should be different. I am so grateful that we get to practice mercy for ourselves during this cold. I am so pleased that we get to practice dying.

And, Ho'oponopono, Ho'oponopono for any living being that is or has experienced suffering of any kind. For all the people and the animals and mother earth herself, for all you who suffer, I am so deeply, deeply sorry and I love you, and the thoughts and memories affecting you, so very, very much.

I know that mankind's suffering is my own suffering. We all share the collective unconscious. It is up to me to heal my own memories, one day at a time. As I work steadily with *Ho'oponopono* I am concentrating on my own path of forgiveness and I believe that touches all souls that desire healing.

Perhaps, sweet reader, you would like to pause and offer yourself *Ho'oponopono* for all your physical suffering during your lifetime!

Steps towards Being Kind to Yourself during Times of Illness
I would like to document the steps I've taken towards healing my own self-rejection and building my self-compassion around illness, hoping that a clarification of the process will be helpful to you.

1. Note your physical symptoms objectively, without stepping in to self-rejection. Simply observe what is going on with your body. My current list, without judgment, is: my tummy feels bloated, my right ear aches, and I have about 40% of my usual energy.
2. If you hear your inner critic begin to offer the "Hitlerian perspective" (which means without mercy, like Hitler) thank your inner critic for sharing and then take a strong stand with your critic. Your stand will sound something like this: "Here's the deal. I *will not* have you speaking to me in this manner. Stop! I do not deserve your meanness. Stop at once and listen to me. What we really need here is kindness not criticism." (This perspective is offered from the wisdom of your inner adult male from the front seat of your car.*) You may not have the experience of facing your inner critic down but you can use the voice you would use if you saw someone abusing a beloved family member, friend or animal.
3. Begin speaking kindly to yourself. If you cannot imagine how you would be tender with yourself, think of how you

---

* See the soul note titled, "The Vehicle of Self Compassion" for an explanation of the front seat.

might speak to a young child or an elderly person you clearly love. Speak to yourself with that same language. This may feel foreign at first. You are building your kindness muscle.
4. Make a list of actions you would take if you loved yourself with deep compassion and true passion. Take these actions daily. Remember, when we are so exhausted, we can hardly speak or move, having an inner adult who is kind and caring truly changes the quality of the time we are ill and encourages either an easier illness or a shorter time span until the body can recover. Here's my list from the recent, exhausting, cold/flu episode that lasted two and a half months.

SELF CARE LIST:
1. See my therapist or check in with my coach to get more ideas on self-care.
2. Check in with a friend daily. .
3. Go to Albuquerque to get RIFE treatments.
4. See my holistic doctor.
5. Go to acupuncturist twice weekly and get herbs.
6. Get lymph drainage or nurturing massage.
7. Cuddle with dog and husband.
8. Take twenty minutes daily for tenderness centering prayer meditation.
9. Get detoxifying footbaths.
10. Remind myself I am dearly and deeply loved.
11. Ask David to be sure he is doing the things he needs to do for himself so that his own self-care is intact and he doesn't get lost in supporting me.
12. Make a list of the people who are capable of offering comfort. Ask them for whatever kind of comfort I can. (i.e. please rub my feet, draw me a hot bubble bath, listen for a

time, hold me, and remind me that I am loved.) If there is no one in your life with whom you can make these requests offer yourself these gifts and make note that it's time to build a larger support system.

Setting up a healing environment with as little stress as possible while you are ill will play a significant role in honoring and caring for yourself while you are sick.

Here are some additional possibilities to consider: Have some reading material available that will support both your physical healing and your emotional well-being. (My favorite inspirational reading is the poetry of Rumi, Hafiz, David Whyte, and Mary Oliver.) If you love great mysteries, biographies or romance novels, keep them on hand. Have your favorite music available to you. Ram Dass's movie on "Fierce Grace" which is about how he recovered from his stroke might provide inspiration. Listening to Stephen and Ondrea Levine's tapes entitled "In the Heart Lies the Deathless" would also be a wonderful way to spend some of your time in repose. It's not necessary, by the way, that you use any of this list. What is of importance is that you have your own list.

In closing, it occurs to me that since I write primarily from my own experience (often from my own ashes) and since I have not yet had to face cancer, or AIDS or heart disease, I cannot write what it is like to be within those very challenging, truly life threatening places. (I have learned much being with dying friends and family with cancer and AIDS among other ailments.) I can say that by being willing to practice dying when I have a common cold, and practice tenderness when my husband has a pinched nerve in his leg, I am building my capacity to be with myself and you, dear reader, in all the things our bodies face as our journey on earth continues.

> I'd like to encourage you to hold an inner marriage ceremony with yourself. Say to yourself in the mirror, "I am with you, dear one, in good times and in bad, in sickness and in health, even death won't part us."

We nurture our physical, emotional, and mental health when we treat ourselves with kindness and caring, especially during times of stress and illness. I invite us all to embrace our own self-love and self-acceptance to help heal our bodies, minds, and spirits. We've been beating ourselves up long enough. Let's treat ourselves with the same tenderness and acceptance we would show toward a loved one when they are sick.

I invite us all to embrace a compassionate way to hold illness, aging and the dying process. Let's use an internal dialogue that is tender, clear, powerful, and healing.

Offering ourselves tenderness when we are ill and being willing to receive tenderness from our loved ones may not decrease our physical suffering at all; the important thing, though, is that when we let our own and one another's love in, we are less alone. Our illness is touched by our own sweet love, our hearts are open and we are connected. This connection gives us more capacity to be present with ourselves within the illness.

I wrote at the beginning of this soul note that for me the biggest tragedy is not losing a spouse through death or divorce, or never finding a mate in the first place. The worst thing that can happen is to abandon or divorce *myself*. That is what I do when I constantly criticize and abuse myself.

As a symbolic commitment to yourself, dear reader, I'd like to encourage you to hold an inner marriage ceremony with yourself. Say to yourself in the mirror, "I am with you, dear one, in good times and in bad, in sickness and in health, even death won't part us."

Being Kind to Yourself When Ill

There is nothing more fulfilling and healing than creating and sustaining a sanctuary inside you, a place where you can go to hold yourself, care for yourself, and love yourself. Knowing how to treat yourself with kindness when you are ill is an important part of *becoming a love dog*. Illness can easily bring with it feelings of impotence both physically and emotionally. Being tender with ourselves means making room for whatever feelings the illness precipitates.

> **Kindness is my only religion.**
> —The Dalai Llama—
> **Within your own illness, mercy is as important as medicine.**
> —Patricia Flasch—

Becoming a Love Dog

> The power of love to change bodies is legendary, built into folklore, common sense, and everyday experience. Love moves the flesh, it pushes matter around. Throughout history, "tender loving care" has uniformly been recognized as a valuable element in healing.
>
> —Larry Dossey—

My Eyes So Soft

Don't
Surrender
Your loneliness so quickly.
Let it cut more
Deep.

Let it ferment and season you
As few human
Or even divine ingredients can.

Something missing in my heart tonight
Has made my eyes so soft,
My voice so
Tender,

My need of God
Absolutely
Clear.

—Hafiz—

Ladinsky, *The Gift, Poems by Hafiz*, copyright 1999. Reprinted with permission.

The Blessing of Core Loneliness

The *love dog* Rumi poem that we used to begin this book tells us that our sadness, loneliness, and grief draw us toward union. Many of us are very familiar with these emotions. In this soul note we will delve more deeply into loneliness.

I've been noticing lately how often I feel lonely, perhaps a third of the time over the past few weeks. Then I realized that loneliness may be a regular visitor these days, at least in part, because I'm in the midst of writing this book and another on *Leaving Your Patterns, Not Your Partners*.

Writing about a topic seems to bring it closer to me. This gives me the opportunity to integrate old emotional issues by observing them, welcoming them, feeling them and then ultimately releasing them. Within this process, I open my heart to you, dear reader, so that you can consider welcoming your own core loneliness.

I'll begin by discussing my own history of loneliness, and I'll invite you to consider doing some journaling around your internal issues of loneliness as well.

I don't really remember exactly when I started feeling lonely. I wonder if the beginning of my loneliness was when the cord was cut as an infant. While I don't have a conscious memory of that feeling of separation out of my mother's womb and into the world, I can imagine that there must have been powerful feelings taking place in this tiny baby girl named Patti.

Then we can skip forward to the age of seven. I don't have very many memories of the times before my father died. I do remember my feeling of connection with him, pining for him, waiting on the porch after school until he drove up in his white Studebaker, and him taking me in his arms and throwing me over his head. I do remember that I knew, unequivocally, that I was loved by my father.

His accidental death when I was seven years old was a turning point on so many different levels for all the members of my family and certainly for me.

What I do remember when he died was that it was like a great hole opened up inside my belly. I began feeling lonely and that feeling remained for many, many years.

I remember nights looking out my bedroom window wondering where he was and why he left. I remember crying myself to sleep. I also remember many sleepless nights while I lay pining for my father and, on some level, missing my mother—the woman she was before he died.

> **The positive intention of my loneliness was that it inspired my inner search. The unresolved pain, even way back then, was driving me to find comfort in some way. I think I already knew it was not available to me from the world outside me.**

Right alongside that feeling of loneliness was a kind of dread, a deep shame. I didn't think I should be feeling like that and I didn't want anyone to know. This, of course, furthered my sense of isolation. I missed him, I missed my mom, and I missed the way our lives had been before he died. I missed my natural connection with God that evaporated when I got the idea that God had taken my dad. My anger shut down my friendship with Christ, which had been natural and very comforting to me up until that time.

I'm hoping that my morning *love dog* sharing has personal redemptive value both for me and for you because I feel exposed and naked, really, to be talking about that time in my life and to be revealing the extent of my loneliness.

The comfort of my paternal grandparents, my sweet Aunt Margaret, and my sister Janice helped me survive the loss; yet the loneliness remained my constant companion. I believe, in looking back, that while it seemed to me it was my beloved father that I missed; an equally significant factor was that I no longer felt connected to God. Christ was no longer my soul companion. Because I lost that sense of solace that came from the place of spiritual alignment, I lost the feeling of who I was. I forgot I was a *love dog*.

I remember a little later along the journey when I was just beginning high school, I used to get to the building when they opened at 5:00 am and go to study hall. What drove me there so early was loneliness and the anxiety I had around that feeling. My home felt like a kind of "after the war" zone or perhaps like we'd experienced a hurricane and when we came back together the key element in our homeostasis as a family had been removed.

I was lonely all through high school. Of course, there were moments of respite when I felt connected to my best friend, when I was engaged in studying, or when I was hanging out with my little sister, Mary. I remember that was the first time I got involved in personal growth. I read *The Power of Positive Thinking* by Norman Vincent Peale eight or ten times in study hall. I was trying to calm the twin demons of loneliness and shame. I didn't know these two emotions ran my life at the time but I did know I had a big black hole inside. I'd read the book and feel a little better for a few days. Then, the old visitors would show up again so I'd reread the book.

The Blessing of Core Loneliness

Let's note here that the positive intention of my loneliness was that it inspired my inner search. The unresolved pain, even way back then, was driving me to find comfort in some way. I think I already knew it was not available to me from the world outside me. The loneliness inspired my path of *becoming a Love Dog*.

I moved away from home, the first time, when I was sixteen. I moved in with eleven other girls and we shared a four-bedroom apartment on Division Street. I got my first job as a secretary in the factory where my father died. I was still lonely. Busier, but lonely. This feeling of "daddy hunger" began playing out when I started spending time with "the much older than I" coach of our baseball team. Now it's obvious to me that I was looking for my daddy in the coach. "Daddy hunger" is one of the more specific ways to describe a primary element of the loneliness I was living with and in.

When I was eighteen, I spent about a year applying for the Peace Corps and jumping through hoops to get in. I was ultimately accepted and sent to Berkeley, California to train to go to Brazil. When we arrived we discovered that we were expected to participate in a language immersion course in Portuguese so no English was spoken. That was unfortunate since I'd had three years of high school Spanish and no training in Portuguese.

I left behind my dream and the Peace Corps within about six weeks. I look back now and I can see that what was driving that decision was that I felt homesick, lonely and isolated. On the one hand, I felt isolated and disconnected in California with the group. On the other hand, this was also my primary feeling at home. I didn't realize then that feelings follow you wherever you go and that there really is no cure "out there," whether it be a new geographical home or the dreamed of "perfect relationship." I didn't have a sustained relationship with my own true self and I had no idea that my own tenderness was what I was searching for.

Becoming a Love Dog

In my first marriage, I was isolated. The man I married hunted, fished, and was actively engaged in sports with most of his time outside of work. I had expected that marriage would allow me to feel connected. I did not know that it was inner work that needed to be done. I expected the marriage itself would fill the hole.

> I'm closing my eyes for a moment to go back inside and imagine kissing that sweet girl and young woman on the forehead. I did not know another way. I'm pausing to bless the one from the past who was so distraught and who needed comforting.

In college and grad school, I was dogged by loneliness. Loneliness and its companion, shame, were deeply ingrained in me by then. Fortunately, I did get professional help. Courtie Fedderson, a gestalt counselor, and Blair Matthews, a Tai Chi master and counselor, provided that first place of sanctuary that helped me to learn to deal with my unresolved loss and depression.

After graduate school, when I began thinking about what I'd do with my master's degree in counseling, I could not imagine becoming part of a system—like the welfare system or the educational system or the medical system. So, I went to Cornucopia, a human potential school and community. Cornucopia provided a reprieve from entering the regular work world.

While my involvement in the community—becoming a seminar leader, traveling around the country giving workshops, and being surrounded by many, many people who were also *love dogs* and offered me large buckets of unconditional love—did much to ease the feeling of loneliness, the core issues, remained. When I look back, I think of the many nights I spent roaming the halls. It felt as if I were looking for something, or someone.

The Blessing of Core Loneliness

The lack of sexual boundaries I had at that time was also related to my desire to avoid loneliness. While it's certainly true that in the late seventies hippy culture many of us were experimenting with sex outside of marriage and having sex with multiple partners, I see that those "experiments," for me, came from a very needy and lost part of myself. Surprisingly, while being with a man in the moment seemed like it would alleviate the loneliness, it actually increased the loneliness and increased the shame I felt about the pain I carried.

It's a bit intense to be writing my own story. I'll pause a moment to offer my younger self some tenderness and comfort.

I'm sorry and I love you, Patricia. I am very sorry about all of your pain and I love you very much. I'm closing my eyes for a moment to go back inside and imagine kissing that sweet girl and young woman on the forehead. I did not know another way. I'm pausing to bless the one from the past who was so distraught and who needed comforting. Please forgive my unconsciousness and thank you for bringing this to my attention.

Perhaps that is, ultimately, what we all long for: our own comfort, our own deep and abiding love for ourselves, and especially kindness for the parts of ourselves that feel broken, untended and raw.

When I kiss the one that still lives inside me who was at study hall at 5:00 am, the one who was so bereft within my first marriage, and the one who lived at Cornucopia roaming the halls at night, my own gentle love helps me to integrate those old visitors who broke my heart. I can, today, integrate those younger aspects of self by giving them a voice, allowing for them, and blessing them. Then this writing becomes a holy, innocent sharing of my own history of loss. It has value to give it voice; first of all because it touches me, and secondly it may touch those who are reading so that they, too, can discover and recover lost parts of themselves.

I'll abbreviate the story of my loneliness for the past thirty years. On the one hand, I have lived an active and purposeful life. My work in private practice and creating trainings has provided me with a kind of fulfillment that I believe few folks have. Connecting with clients and teaching them how to have more intimacy within themselves and in their own relationships has been as healing for me as I believe it's been for them.

> I've come to realize that loneliness for me, is both a core pattern, a kind of spell I slip into, *and* it is a loneliness for something much deeper; it is my longing for God.

On the other hand, it's loneliness that drove me to make a career choice that would allow for so much connection. I needed, and still do need, the connection that comes from doing soul work with other *love dogs*.

In my life I have touched my own "dark side." I have gone far into my own depth. That is the most essential gift I offer clients today. Consciously or unconsciously, the ones who walk into my practice *know* that I will have the capacity to be with their depth, their suffering and their un-integrated parts of self. Because I can do that, they also know I will be able to help them reveal and come to cherish their gifts and greatness as well.

There is one more aspect of loneliness I'll bring to this writing now. I can see that, within the context of my current marriage, I chose a partner who is incredibly loyal and has the capacity to stay for the long haul. After fifteen attempts at long-term relationship, I discovered that I needed someone who could provide stability and continuity. The biggest qualities that I was looking for in a man were:

- Willingness. He would give his heart to looking within himself and into our partnership so that we could resolve all the barriers to intimacy. Another way of describing this would be a partner with a high interest in personal growth.
- Spiritual capacity. He would have a spiritual path that was already deeply established and an interest in expanding that path through life. It wasn't, by the way, religion that was the criteria for my choice. Rather having a path that he'd defined with a God of his own understanding. I didn't know it then, but I was looking for another *love dog*.
- A spiritual, emotional, practical, and financial skill set. In other words, someone who loved "God" as he defined "God," was interested in personal growth, and had the practical skills to make his way in the world. (My husband David's primary profession, for over fifty years, was an accountant.)

I did not want to be the parent in any of the above arenas. I did want to attract a partner. This list represented my own inner criteria for choosing a partner. That doesn't mean these criteria would work for you. Do consider, though, giving them some thought and perhaps coming up with a list of what it is that really matters to you. If you define yourself as a *love dog*, partnering with another who craves a profound connection with self and the Divine will be helpful.

Those were my *conscious* intentions in creating the partnership with David.

My *unconscious* intention was to appease loneliness, to find someone who could comfort me, to find someone who would be devoted to our relationship and be able to "stay" through all the storms that long-term marriage brings up.

I used to be ashamed that loneliness, in large part, motivated my choice of marriage partner and my choice to be in long term marriage. Now, I just see that loneliness had a positive intention. The positive intention of my loneliness and longing is "to connect more deeply with myself, other *love dogs*, and God."

Here are a few more thoughts on loneliness before we close. There have been countless times in our marriage that I am lying in David's arms feeling incredibly lonely. His presence, in and of itself, cannot abate loneliness. I've come to realize that loneliness for me is both a core pattern, a kind of spell I slip into, *and* it is a loneliness for something much deeper; it is my longing for God.

Often, when David or another close intimate of mine is away traveling, I begin to pine. As the time of separation lengthens, it may surely feel like I miss David, or Amba, or Stephi; but the deeper issue is that I miss myself. I miss God. I miss my own comfort. I long for God. I long for that sense of deep connection with Source that seems to have slipped through my fingers. I also miss Patricia. I miss the feeling of being emotionally connected to me. It seems as if I am an empty vessel and tenderness has slipped out of my hands.

Many, many times through the years I have felt utterly abandoned by God both because I have my little one's pining for God (the parents I lost and the connection with Christ I lost at seven) and because I made the assumption that when I am going through great difficulty, God dropped my hand.

I always come to discover that it's me that drops God's hand and not the other way around. God, Presence, Source truly never leaves me. The spell I've entered, though, convinces me that I am utterly alone.

God, as I've defined God today, is a God called *Tenderness* and lives in the well-spring of my being no matter what human condition is passing through me. This Tender God loves me in all my loneliness, shame, despair—in all of it. This Tender God is teaching me how to comfort myself today.

The Blessing of Core Loneliness

> Yet, if we continue to run we lose the possibility of befriending a part of ourselves that has truly been longing for our love. This writing is another call to "embrace our shadows."

I believe it's honorable for neediness and loneliness to be among the reasons for choosing a spouse or a long-term commitment. I also believe that having loneliness be the *only* reason for being together won't preserve the connection or set the relationship up for a lasting run. I know that when loneliness is driving our lives and making our choices *unconsciously,* that very unconsciousness defeats our potential for self-integration and self-realization. If I am in denial of my core motivation, I cut off my capacity for soul connection within myself and with my partner.

The healing of loneliness, the integration of it into our own being, is an internal job. A partner cannot protect us from our own depth and a partner cannot cover for God.

Today my longing for God is one of my absolutely favorite aspects of who I am. I see that I am *always, always,* either feeling connected to the God of Tenderness *or* I am longing for that connection. My longing for God, as my favorite poet, Rumi, says *is my connection with God.* Like the dog's moaning for its master, my longing for God *is* the return message.

Let's pause for a moment and consider all the things we do to avoid loneliness. Think of how many times you have used drugs, alcohol, or food to avoid feeling lonely. Think of all the times you have hung out with others just to avoid being alone. Think of the energy extension that goes on in an effort to avoid loneliness. It's almost like being chased by a tiger.

Stopping to face the tiger, in my own experience, is actually less painful. For those of us who have been raised in homes where feelings, all feelings, were to be avoided at all costs, stopping to face the tiger is a frightening prospect. It's familiar to keep running and it's both unfamiliar and uncomfortable to stop running.

Yet, if we continue to run, we lose the possibility of befriending a part of ourselves that has truly been longing for our love. This writing is another call to "embrace our shadows."

Let's also think for a moment about all of the coping mechanisms we may be using to keep loneliness at bay. Perhaps we're over working, or over achieving, or over doing any one thing, and camouflaging our soft underbelly. (Not, by the way, that I'm saying work or achievement *are* an avoidance of core issues, but rather, they *could* be.) Each of us would have to take our own inner inventory to find out what is true for us.

Perhaps we're going from one partner to the next—or staying in a relationship that feels dead—just to keep away from l-o-n-e-l-y.

This soul note is an invitation to exploration. What's going on? And, what would happen if we paused and allowed for our own loneliness or shame or whatever other core issue has been dogging us? What if we just let it in?

I'm lonely, LONELY, L O N E L Y. I'm as lonely as anyone I've ever known. Loneliness is one of my top ten oldies playing sometimes softly and sometimes loudly in the background of my mind for hours, days and nights on end. I feel like making a neon sign and hanging it on my forehead, "Loneliness frequently visits here."

> **What a holy thing to know about this voice of loneliness and longing. I want this voice to be part of my choir. Ultimately, I want ALL the voices in the choir to be heard. Together, singing in harmony, they make one beautiful song.**

Loneliness is not a definition of *who I really am*. It is, however, a frequent visitor to this *love dog*.

Yes, and I've now been naked with my readers and I've

The Blessing of Core Loneliness

survived it. In fact, b*ringing boldness to loneliness cuts the shame in half.* I often have a judgment of my written work: that it's too raw and that it *should* be more clinical, safer. I should spend more time writing about case studies than exploring my own psyche. Yet this raw place is perhaps just another authentic expression of what goes on with this one soul. My own vulnerability keeps me true to my written word and to you. I believe I'm not alone.

I believe that most, maybe even all of you, have been dogged by loneliness, or shame or fear or rage; some sense that there is a black hole living inside of you the size of the Grand Canyon. Perhaps there is a comfort in knowing you are not alone. I want to touch hearts by opening completely to my own loneliness, in and of itself, and will not be sharing stories of anyone else's loneliness in this soul note.

I mentioned in the soul note, "When Food becomes a Substitute for Love," Robert Bly's concept of the "long bag we drag behind us." The idea is that we are all given an invisible bag when we are born. We place in that bag the emotions we don't want to feel and the parts of ourselves we find unlovable. As we age we keep throwing more and more unacceptable parts into the bag and it gets bigger and heavier. It may get so heavy we can't carry it anymore. At some point in our lives, we might be forced to stop and look in the bag. When we spend our lives refusing to look into that black bag, it's a bit like being invited to a feast and refusing to sample some of the dishes. Being willing to taste all the dishes, experience all that we are, certainly makes for a richer experience.

It's scary, certainly at first, to begin looking at what's in that long bag. But, as time goes on, and we keep looking, it gets easier. We begin to get some perspective on this pouch and its contents. There is a kind of inherent richness that comes along with exploration in the bag. I am more, not less, for knowing about my loneliness. I am closer to myself and also closer to you. I have touched a part of myself that felt unlovable and now just feels true. It also feels innocent. What a holy thing to know about this voice of loneliness and longing. What a wondrous thing to see that my loneliness is part of me and reflects my *love dog* nature.

I want this voice to be part of my choir. Ultimately, I want *all* the voices in the choir to be heard. Together, singing in harmony, they make one beautiful song. In my years as a student of countless seminars, I have never been able to stand the teachers that teach from the perspective of, "I'm an expert. I have it handled. I am top dog," etc. The ones I love most are the ones who are most vulnerable. The ones who stand in a circle with me looking at their own long bags are the ones that truly lift me.

I have loved and comforted that lonely place within me in many different ways. One of the most effective and transformative has been the process of *Ho'oponopono* that I have used often in this book (Len and Vitale, *Zero Limits*). *Ho'oponopono* would be an excellent way to comfort yourself within your own history of loneliness so that you can bless it, forgive it, release it and then offer that same blessing to all those you touch. Make it a practice to feel the loneliness that you have been running from all these years, and love it. I recommend using a journal to record your thoughts, feelings, and memories of isolation. Then try giving yourself the gift of *Ho'oponopono*. You might begin something like this:

To the lonely child in my belly: I'm so sorry, I love you. I'm so sorry for the times I felt isolated, and alone. For the times I felt I had no friends, I'm sorry, I love you. To all those memories of pain, when I felt I had nowhere to turn, I'm so sorry, I love you. To the memories of a home where I felt so little love and no comfort, I'm so sorry, I love you. To the memories of my youth, when I felt different and isolated, I'm so sorry, I love you. To each and every moment of loneliness I have felt in the intervening years, I'm so sorry, I love you. For all the lonely parts of myself in the past and all the lonely parts that remain today

The Blessing of Core Loneliness

Ho'oponopono, I'm sorry and I love you.

Thank you for bringing this to my attention for healing. I offer all these memories to the Universe for transformation.

And, for all the lonely parts of you, my dear reader, past and present, *Ho'oponopono. I'm so sorry and I love you very, very much.*

A Blessing of Core Emotions

Within me lives
a core of loneliness,
running like a river,
in the center of my being.

Within me lies
every fear anyone ever had
since the miracle of our creation.

Within me lives
all the shame anyone ever experienced
since time began.

Within me lies
all the rage anyone ever felt.

Within me lives
all the worry anyone ever had
since the beginning of time.

WITHIN ME LIES
ALL OF OUR HEARTBREAKING HUMANITY

—Patricia Flasch—

Sometimes I fly like an eagle. Sometimes I'm deep in despair.

—John Denver—

> The most powerful weapon on earth is the human soul on fire.
>
> —F. Foch—

The Soul of Relationship Beyond Our Patterns

There lives a place in each of us, at the very center of our being, that has been untouched by *anything*—a sweet place in the Great Silence which we often call "Self" or "Soul." This same sweet place lives in the center of our soul relationships. I often explain this using the example of a triangle. In my marriage with David, we sit at the base of the triangle, at the points. So, David's Self is on one point and my Self is at the other. The tip of the triangle is Spirit and our essential and eternal relationship with Spirit. The tip of the triangle is the guiding force and ultimate Source of connectedness. It is the "glue" that holds the spirit of our relationships together. That is the place we return to after each wave of human conditioning works its way through us. The tip of the triangle informs and connects the entire triangle.

This place of "Soul" is free of all of our human conditioning. It is beyond all of our wounding, regrets, grief, anger, fear, shame; it is, in truth, beyond our humanity, connected with our spark of divinity. Jesus calls this place The Center of Our Love, Buddhists call this place the Dharma, Hindus call it Atman, Theologians call it Soul, and Psychologists call it the Psyche.

The Soul of Relationships Beyond Our Patterns

In that place of *grace*, it doesn't matter what we do, where we live, or what we own or how we look; it only matters how we feel connected to the Infinite. While we often live in a place where our human conditioning continues to arise and grey over or tarnish that place of sweetness, beneath it all, our essential nature emerges once again. We touch wholeness and we, once again, remember Who We Really Are (*love dogs*).

When I do visualizations with clients at the end of our sessions I like to remind them that the sun does not go away on a cloudy day. The sun is always there and it rises again and again and again. In any kind of inclement weather it lives behind the clouds and storms. The sun *is*. Our connection with the Divine *is*. And, in our emotional body, it often feels—really *feels*—like we are disconnected. The spiritual truth is we cannot disconnect from that which we *are*.

There is a wonderful prayer and song from the Jewish tradition with the lovely refrain:

> Return again, Return Again, Return to the Land of Your Soul.
> Return to who you are. Return to what you are.
> Return to where you are, born and reborn again.
>
> Robbie and Judith Gass sing my favorite version.

In the midst of relationship with our human beloveds, this same process continues to unfold as it does within our individual psyche. There are times in my marriage, that sometimes last for days and days, that seem like forever, when we are both unconsciously operating out of our human condition. Perhaps we are not in our conditioning constantly during those days. Maybe we pop out for a few moments or a few hours; still we are going through a "dark" time in our individual and collective humanity. This may look like a power struggle. Perhaps we don't agree on a direction in our lives. Perhaps we don't agree on a way of preparing for the future Perhaps we don't agree about a financial decision. No matter the outside event, internally we feel disconnected. There seems to be a wall of separation in our coupleship.

> **When I go into what I'm really feeling, a kind of alchemical shift happens. Just in saying my emotional truth, the inner gate opens. Revealing what is truly going on in me lifts the shame and opens the door for connection.**

Just a few days ago I was saying to my life partner David, "I miss God, I miss myself, and I miss you. I feel disconnected and disengaged. I'm lonely and I have this deep sense of longing. It feels like the light within me has gone out and I'm fumbling around in the darkness. I feel bereft and abandoned." And, as always, when I go into what I'm really feeling, a kind of alchemical shift happens. Just in saying my emotional truth, the inner gate opens. Revealing what is truly going on in me lifts the shame and opens the door for connection.

Now we will begin a discussion of what's possible beyond those times of power struggle, disconnect, and longing. Following is a journal entry from August 2006 that reflects the spark of mutual connection in my marriage with David. For this soul note, I've chosen to offer this journal entry, which is a story from my own marriage, as a final gift without making reference to other love dog *relationships.*

Just now we are traveling on the Sunshine Coast in British Columbia. We are about fifty miles north of Vancouver camping in a provincial park surrounded by mature oak, redwood, cedar, ferns, and sycamore trees. The ocean is lapping at the shore in the

The Soul of Relationships Beyond Our Patterns

background. This campground feels holy. We've been here about three weeks. This is a working vacation for me. I spend three days a week working with clients by phone and then take luxurious four-day weekends.

When my partner wakes me each morning, he brings me a cup of tea. I lie on our airbed with all the tent windows open watching the trees through the ceiling screen. I lie in the trees offering soul and business coaching to my clients. Coaching from the woods is a unique experience. It's a bit like the trees are participating in the coaching so each session has a feeling of grace and expansion that feels fresh. This spaciousness brings added wisdom to each connection time with a client. It's really quite awesome.

Just yesterday I spoke with a client from the Ukraine. I also worked with a couple from Boston—one of whom was in Boston calling and the other who called from New York—meeting me by teleconference in the woods in British Columbia. Then I had a session with two clients from Santa Monica and closed my day working with a long-term client from Santa Fe.

I am so utterly blessed. So completely blessed. I get to work in a grove of trees, with the sounds of the ocean in the background, with my sweet husband available for support and my beloved "puppa" (puppy dog) at my side. It doesn't get better than this.

Later in the morning David brings me breakfast and the puppy hops up on the bed for cuddling. As the coaching continues, my partner takes the laundry in to town, takes himself to a coffee shop, and does a Sudoku puzzle. He returns to the campsite just prior to lunchtime and we share a walk through the woods, a wonderful salad, and a twenty-minute centering prayer meditation.

These days we speak softly to one another. There is a kind of wordless communion taking place as I do my part to provide for us and he does his part to nurture us. We are happy, deeply happy.

The afternoon follows the pattern of the morning and

around 5:00 or 6:00 pm we meet up again and have a partnership conversation about what would *feed us both* for the evening. That may be a trip to the local pub for dinner and a few games of cards. It may be a walk on the beach and a quick swim followed by dinner in town. Or, it may be we cook at the campsite, play some games, read, and tend to the needs of our old puppa.

As the evening comes to a close we share about what touched us in the day, what challenged us, what surprised us, what moved us. We listen quietly to one another's soul stories. Later, just before lights out, we read stories to one another. Just now those stories are coming from a delightful book by Rachel Naomi Remen, *Kitchen Table Wisdom*.

David is getting sleepy by this time while I am frequently awake another hour or two. So, I often do some self-soothing aloud so that I can complete my day with my inner child by listening to her and offering her comfort. Sometimes David dozes off during this time, sometimes he listens. If he's already lost in dreamtime, I may journal or do a bit of yoga or let my romance novel soothe me to sleep.

We spoon most of the night, *love dog* to *love dog*, husband and wife. If I have a bad dream I am always welcome to awaken David so that I can talk about it. Sometimes, though, I am content to sit and listen to the puppa and the sweet man snoring, knowing we can talk about the dream later.

> I'm allowing you to get a picture of what lives beyond our conditioning, the kind of creativity that spills out when we are internally connected and operating from the true depth and strength of our partnership.

While we've been here on the Sunshine Coast, we've decided to invest in some real estate. While we are not planning on moving here any time soon, perhaps we will move here when I retire. The decision to invest feels intuitive and effortless. It just came to us while we are here. Though we've often talked, through the years, about spending some of our retirement time in Canada, we had no idea we were ready to back up those thoughts with a real estate purchase.

If we decide to move here one day, David could have lots of opportunity to be involved in local politics. He enjoys the utter friendliness of the people; he adores being so near the ocean; he loves the local pubs and coffee shops, and the funky feeling of this small town. All of my life, I have had a dream to live near the ocean, within walking distance to shops, library, and movies. I want to live in a culture that is politically liberal and I truly love the lack of violence in Canada. Since David has dual citizenship (English and Canadian) we are also interested in the possibility of retiring in Canada. The socialized medicine here would greatly increase our feeling of ease in our later years.

We meet our realtor at the very first open house we attend. Ted turns out to be an easy friend and skillful realtor. He listens very well to what we say as he takes us to see eight or ten properties. On our third day together, we find *it*.

Once we've decided to purchase a property, we easily slip into the things we do best. For starters, I get to choose the property. I am very specific about what it is that will make me happy in a home and I really need to have the feeling of a spiritual sanctuary in order to thrive. We have learned through the years that if I love it, it will automatically serve David's needs. It will be beautiful and he will love it.

We also know, if left to David's perspective—since he likes to have a kind of global look at things—we might view 100 homes and he would look at all the possibilities in each home to see how it might work. After a while that gets to be overkill and in our current situation it just won't work since we only have a few days to make our selection. I generally *know* if I want to buy a home when I walk in the foyer. We are in complete agreement on this decision about allowing me to choose. This time I have decided on a beautiful, almost new condo just two blocks from the ocean that overlooks Gibson's Bay and is walking distance to the library and the town, with a lovely view of the sea.

We also agree that I'll do what I do best: create the relationship with the realtor and communicate clearly what it is that we want. David will begin networking in the community so that he can find the lawyer, banker, notary, property manager, and mortgage broker we might like to hire. David is a master networker. Throughout the transaction I continue to build relationships and David continues to create our resources. We work together at the bargaining table to get the deal we feel is best.

After these twenty-four years together we operate as a finely tuned instrument. Once the home is selected David handles most of the financial dealings. He's the lead on creating where we'll get the financing, how we'll structure the mortgage, how we'll create the tenant, etc., He is able to find an interest-only mortgage which means we won't have to make huge payments while the equity is building in the property.

We are an awesome creative team. I believe that we are probably part of the top 5% most creative couples in the world. I'm not meaning to brag. I'm just observing our soul skills, our innate talents operating in tandem. I'm allowing you to get a picture of what lives beyond our conditioning, the kind of creativity that spills out when we are internally connected and operating from the true depth and strength of our partnership.

At the credit union in British Columbia, the team was laughing with us on our last day, calling us the "whirlwind staff." They said they'd never seen a couple create a home with such speed and efficiency. It really was only ten days between the moment we met Ted and the day we signed the papers to purchase the property and met our new tenant.

The Soul of Relationships Beyond Our Patterns

A closing fun story: Our *love dog* friends Amba and Chittak are coming from Santa Fe to spend the weekend with us here in the Canadian redwoods. Since the weekend is a very busy holiday weekend on the Sunshine Coast, we had a concern that they may not get the campsite right next to us. We decided to reserve the adjacent campsite by renting it the night before they would actually arrive. The campground was full by 5:00 pm. David's creativity shone again as he sublet the adjacent campsite to someone needing a spot for the one night before our friends would arrive.

Another favorite example of David's creativity occurred many years ago. We decided to take three months off and go to Jasper and Banff in western Canada. We thought that financing the trip would be easier if we got our mortgage at home covered. So, we brainstormed about how we would get a good tenant while we traveled. David came up with the idea that since the pope was visiting Denver during the summer, perhaps we could rent the house to the pope's people. He called the Vatican and spoke to the Director for Public Relations for the Denver visit and arranged to rent our home to the pope's advance publicity team. Not only was our mortgage completely paid, we received an additional $2000 bonus.

These examples of how we work together soul-to-soul are lovely to share.

However, I do want to make myself completely clear. When you have devoted your relationship to soul healing, which is what *love dogs* do, then whether we are going through what we often call "dark times" or whether we are "dancing in the light," all of the time we spend with one another has value for our souls.

It's not my purpose to celebrate the "good times" and put up with the "bad times."

That view is dualistic and, in and of itself, causes suffering. Rather, it is my purpose to live in authenticity and to honor the old visitors that come in the form of anger, hurt, guilt, fear, grief, or despair. I intend to know that they arise as messengers to ask, "Are you going to love me now?" I will ask myself, "Can I find a place within that is tender towards myself when I am angry or frightened?" When I do this, the place of "Soul" touches my humanity. I return to my true self as a *love dog*.

Also, "Can I find a way to love David in all of his humanity? Can I bless this man when he's defensive or stuck or cranky and not just when he meets my models and I feel like dancing?" There are moments when I can do just that. And there are also many moments when, though I can bless him, I think it would be "better" to be connected. And then there are countless times when I judge and fight with our human condition and the way it expresses itself between us. That is my definition of Hell.

I truly intensify my suffering anytime I judge "what is" and try to get it to go away rather than accepting it. When I can come from the perspective that it's all a blessing, the whole range, the entire experience, that we came here to make one another's rough stone smooth, then the amount of time I spend internally connected is greater and the darkness actually blends into the light. This is the place of grace!

Have you ever had what we call "a good cry," the kind of crying that becomes a filling up and spilling over of the heart, the kind of weeping that is met with a deep allowance? If you've had that experience, then you know, once the tears are shed, something completes inside and its time for a nap, a walk in the park, or an ice cream. This is what it's like with all of our feelings. If we allow for them and allow for the process they bring up—stop fighting them and, instead, surrender—then those tears, as we allow for them inside our selves, become our bridge to one another. This is the place of love.

I know a common way to perceive our relationships is to make a kind of laundry list of the qualities we love in our partners and then a second list of the things we despise and, therefore, want to change in our partners. (We often have this same conditional love list in our relationship with ourselves.) This is a limited view.

A more expansive view is, "I love you, Patricia, however you are. I embrace your whole range. I accept your diversity. I appreciate your aliveness. And, David, I love you in your wholeness and in your seemingly broken parts." When we say, "I do" to the cranky, wounded ones they can relax in us because they know they are welcome.

When we say, "I hate you. Get out. Get lost" they fight back. They get louder. They are stubborn.

Accepting and blessing everything is a living practice, an authenticity practice. Countless times we forget how to love ourselves and one another; then we remember. I encourage you to use the tools presented in this book, or find others that work for you, to build more caring relationships with others and yourself. If I look back I see that the percentage of time I spend loving myself today is much, much larger than it was decades ago. And, the time in my marriage when I am either deeply loving David or accepting our wounded places is growing and growing.

Join me in taking a stand for the path of authenticity in our marriages to ourselves and to one another. As we do that practice, we walk in beauty. There is a Native American chant on a CD by my dear friend, Lisanne Hawkes that goes, "May beauty be before me. May beauty be behind me. May beauty be below me. May beauty be above me. May beauty be beside me. May beauty be inside me. May beauty be all around me."

My heart's desire for you, my *love dog* friend, is that you may also discover the glorious possibilities that live beyond your patterns.

Thank you for listening.

> In our homes and in our hearts ***PARTNERSHIP RULES***.
>
> —Patricia Flasch & David Pease—

> The voice of the river that has emptied into the ocean,
> Now laughs and sings just like God.
>
> —Hafiz—

Conclusion

I feel so blessed as I reread this book, *Becoming a Love Dog, From Emptiness to Tenderness*. It's hard to describe. I feel as if I were born to write this book, yet its being written to me as much as through me. It is my dharma as the Buddhist's say, or my Service as the Christians say, BUT more than that, my own soul is healed out of my deep desire to offer you, dear reader, these words and skills so that you may find your own way Home.

It's as if I'm sitting in the midst of a lovely garden that was planted lifetimes ago. I get to bask in the garden *and* I'm inviting the most willing souls on earth, the *love dogs*, to come join me. Together we enjoy the garden; together we pull the weeds; together we reap the harvest.

In rereading this book one last time before it goes to final edit, I am struck by how the very writing of it; the putting my heart on paper has been a transformative experience. I know that this book will be of service. I hope you can relate to the stories and, at the same time, *know* that we are not our stories. We are that which lives beyond our stories. Though we think we lose our connection with the Divine, we are in the midst of that connection *always*.

While writing the soul note **Separation Anxiety**, I shared how

The Soul of Relationships Beyond Our Patterns

I was impacted by my own losses. In this new level of ownership of my fear of being alone, I discovered what's on the other side: my capacity to both treasure my own company and make more room inside for the times when I fear being alone. I have offered you the opportunity of learning both about your own separation anxiety and what is on the other side for you.

While writing **The Vehicle of Self-Compassion**, my personal capacity to be kind to myself has grown. I am kinder to myself than I was prior to the writing and I am more skillful in moving around my car. This impacts everyone I touch because I am also kinder to them. I offer you this way of shifting towards kindness in yourself. It's my life's truest work to be as kind to myself as I would to my most beloved friend, and it continues to be a work "of progress, not perfection."

While writing **Developing Inner Authority**, I kept in mind, and close to my heart, the thousands of students and clients I have been privileged to work with through the years. It is so important for all of us to develop the skill to find answers to our questions inside our own beings. This soul note was written to support each of us in our quest to find our own unique truth, path, and song.

The soul note **Walking through Grief** was meant to pay tribute to the countless friends and mentors who have stood at my side during my own grief. I hope this soul note opens a place in you where you can find more hands and hearts to link with in your own grief and come to know more ways that you can self-soothe when you are grieving.

The soul note entitled **When Food Becomes a Substitute for Love** gave me an opportunity to share many layers of my own suffering around food, diet, and body image. I share my story in the trust that it will open you to your own story and the healing within it. I know that I am not alone in this age-old pain. I hope this soul note is a balm for your heartache around food, weight, and appearance; that it offers you mercy in your pain, and puts hope in your heart.

In the chapter on **The Tyranny of Urgency**, I suggested a frame of reference where you might discover how much of your life is fueled by adrenalin and operating on DEADlines. The writing offers another perspective that includes how one goes about stepping away from urgency towards tranquility.

When I wrote the section on **Effort vs. Inspiration**, it actually shifted the way I was writing the book. I reminded myself, once again, to stop trying so hard and just let the voices of the *Ones I Hold Most Dear* speak through my pen.

I used the model from *The Power of Full Engagement* by Loehr and Schwartz to finish the final draft. All day long I've balanced ninety minutes of writing followed by thirty to sixty minutes of swimming or novel reading, or playing ball with my puppy. I feel "full" but I don't feel pushed, and I am so much closer to completing the writing project than I thought possible. Can you hold your "To Do List" more lightly? I'd love for this soul note to encourage you to live from inspiration.

Rereading my work on **Being Kind to Yourself When Ill** opened my heart again to a whole new level of tenderness for myself when I'm ill. It's a wonderful fact that when we become more compassionate towards ourselves, we automatically offer more compassion to all we meet on the path. This chapter is my encouragement, to each of you, to consider a kinder way to treat yourself when you are struggling physically or emotionally.

I love rereading **The Blessing of Core Loneliness**. It's paradoxical, really, to have started this writing thinking, "I must be nuts to make myself so vulnerable in front of the world," and I've ended it thinking, "Wow, I feel blessed to be this soul, this *love dog* who can write about such personal feelings with such self-compassion and kindness. And, I am offering words of a never-ending love for all of you, my sister and brother *love dogs*."

Sharing about **The Soul of Relationship Beyond Our Patterns** refreshed my awareness of my own *love dog* affair with my life partner, David. It also became a tribute to all those couples I have been privileged to spend time with—throughout my three decades as a psycho-spiritual counselor—as they work through their relationship issues. I honor their grief, fear, anger, *and* their soft tears, sweet smiles and ways of finding their way back to one another or coming to terms with letting go. Finally, I celebrate that beyond our patterns our relationship with our deepest selves remains robustly intact despite what we go through in our heartbreaking humanity.

It is my deep prayer that this collection of soul notes on *Becoming a Love Dog* will help you celebrate yourself and be compassionate towards yourself. I hope that my journey to uncover my own inner *love dog* inspires you to live more as the *love dog* that you are.

Becoming a Love Dog

I Knew We Would be Friends

As soon as you opened your mouth
And I heard your soft
Sounds,

I knew we would be
Friends.

The first time, dear pilgrim, I heard
You laugh,

I knew it would not take me long
To turn you back into
God.

—Hafiz—

(Ladinsky, *The Subject Tonight is Love - 60 Wild and Sweet Poems of Hafiz*. Reprinted with permission.)

References

Barks, Coleman, and Michael Green, trans. *The Illuminated Rumi*. New York: Broadway Books, a division of Bantam, Doubleday, Dell Publishing, 1997.

Barks, Coleman, and John Moyne, trans. *The Essential Rumi*. New York: HarperCollins, 1995.

Barks, Coleman, trans. *The Soul of Rumi: A New Collection of Ecstatic Poems*. San Francisco: Harper, 2001.

Cameron, Julia. *The Artist's Way: A Spiritual Path to Higher Creativity*. New York: Jeremy P. Tarcher/Putnam 2002.

———. *The Vein of Gold*. New York: Jeremy P. Tarcher/Putnam, 1997.

Ladinsky, Daniel, trans. *The Subject Tonight is Love – 60 Wild and Sweet Poems of Hafiz*. New York: Pumpkin House Press, 1996.

———. *Love Poems From God: Twelve Sacred Voices from the East and West*. New York: Penguin, 2002.

———. *The Gift: Poems by Hafiz*. New York: Penguin, 1999.

Len, Dr. Ihaleakala Hew, and Joe Vitale. *Zero Limits, The Secret Hawaiian System for Wealth, Health, Peace, and More*. Hoboken, NJ: John Wiley & Sons, 2007.

Loehr, James, and Tony Schwartz. *The Power of Full Engagement*. New York: The Free Press, 2003.

Maslow, Abraham. *Toward a Psychology of Being*. Hoboken, NJ: John Wiley & Sons, 1998.

Muller, Wayne. *Legacy of the Heart: The Spiritual Advantage of a Painful Childhood*. New York: Fireside, 1992.

Whyte, David. *Where Many Rivers Meet: Poems by David Whyte*. Many Rivers Press, 1990.

Information on Patricia's Latest Offerings

Quarterly Love Dog Newsletter
Sign up free on www.BecomingaLoveDog.com

For additional copies of
Becoming a Love Dog - From Emptiness to Tenderness
Order for $15.95 through www.Amazon.com

Round Women - Retrieving the Shadow of Women's Bodies
A booklet of Patricia's poetry
Download for $6.95 from www.BecomingaLoveDog.com

Workshops and Performances

Please check www.BecomingaLoveDog.com
for information on Patricia's upcoming events.

If you would like to contact Patricia about a private session intensive, a custom designed seminar, book signing, or lecture in your area you can reach her at:

Patricia S. Flasch, MS

2503 Calle de Rincon Bonito

Santa Fe, New Mexico 87505

phoenix@patriciaflasch.com

phone: 505-438-8905

fax: 505-438-2423

About the Author

Patricia Flasch has always been fascinated by **the discovery of soul**. Her career as counselor, mentor, coach, and soul friend began when she was nine years old and her friends and neighbors would come by her house and pay her a nickel for her talents. Given her passion for how people connect, Patricia earned her Bachelor's Degree in Communications (1978). After receiving her Master's in Counseling from the University of Wisconsin (1980), Patricia entered a human potential training program called Cornucopia in St. Mary, KY, and became a national seminar leader and the marketing director for that organization.

Following her years at Cornucopia, Patricia ran a private counseling practice for six years in Seattle, WA. Her phenomenally successful program was called Personal Mastery Training.

Upon leaving Seattle, Patricia and her husband David moved to Denver, CO, and opened an organization called Leading from the Heart, which she sustained for the next decade and where she also received training as a non-denominational, new thought minister.

Her next adventure was to move to Santa Fe, NM, where she has resided for the past eleven years. Patricia attended a variety of leading edge coaching schools such as Coachville, Coach University, and Coach Training Institute.

Her lifelong spiritual purpose is to reveal the presence of grace to soul seekers through private counseling, workshops, and writing.

Endorsements

Through this writing Patricia shows us a way to "fetch'" our inner love dog. Full of tips for life and beautiful heart-stretching poetry. A life changing read.

Susan Rush, Spiritual Companion, Santa Fe, NM

There is strength of simplicity, complexity, and depth in the manner you convey all in this book. I felt under a spell.

Karen DiTrapani, Shamanic Coach

What I liked was learning that anguish has a sacred purpose.

Ashisha Mercer, Mothering Magazine

When Patricia works with me, I'm clear on where I stand and at the same time ready to start a new dance.

Gail Gang, Painter and Gardening Coach

Patricia is the way of the mirror for me and for so many. There is no one who has ever given me the glimpse, allowed the inklings to emerge and flower, as she has.

Michael Nicola, Realtor

Printed in the United States
219543BV00001B/1/P